Wallace-Homestead
Price Guide to

AMERICAN
COUNTRY
ANTIQUES

Wallace-Homestead
Price Guide to

AMERICAN
COUNTRY
ANTIQUES

EIGHTH EDITION

DON & CAROL RAYCRAFT

Wallace-Homestead Book Company
Radnor, Pennsylvania

Library of Congress Catalog Card Number 86-640023
ISBN-0-87069-503-7

Designed by Tony Jacobson
Manufactured in the United States of America

2 3 4 5 6 7 8 9 0   7 6 5 4 3 2 1 0 9 8

Contents

Acknowledgments

We appreciate the hard work and the friendship of numerous people who helped in the preparation of this time-consuming and demanding project. For their assistance in putting together the eighth edition, we thank the following individuals and enterprises:

Teri and Joe Dziadul
Linda Grunewald
John and Mary Purvis
Paul Brisco
Gary Guyette and Julia/Guyette
　　Inc.
Charlie DeKoninck
Bobby B. Wahrenburg
Bruce Lube
Country Hearth
Alex Hood
Edna M. Faulkner
Joe and Opal Pickens
Don and Betty Gangloff
Corwin Roop
Al Behr
Mr. and Mrs. Richard Zanetti

Sara Ashley
J. H. Knight
Wayne Leinback
Martha Smith
Libby Kilkelly
Brent Gearhart
Dothan Boothe
Kaye Crabill
L. C. Beckerdite
Mark Grove
Elizabeth Bright
Ken and Carllene Elliott
Larry Detwiler
Dan Lomax
Mondella Wunder
D. P. Kotarba
Cindy Smith

Photography Credits

Carol Raycraft
Joseph Dziadul
Owens Studio
Linda Grunewald

Jim Hughes
Bruce Lube
R. Craig Raycraft

Introduction

In the past year we have had the opportunity to speak at antiques shows and seminars in Pennsylvania, Oregon, New York, Virginia, North Carolina, and Illinois. Invariably the first question that comes up is, "Where can I still find good country things at reasonable prices?"

Finding Country Antiques

We have a friend who lost his job after almost twenty years of employment with a company that makes tractors. He had been a semiserious collector of painted furniture and folk art over the years and decided, after some deliberation, to become a

Nest of seven lathe-turned maple bowls, early twentieth century. **$400–$450**

serious "picker." A *picker* is an individual whose livelihood comes from finding something, writing a check, locating a buyer, and selling the item before his own check clears the bank. A picker who wants to feed himself and at least two of his dependents must have a broad knowledge of the antiques market and a trusty road map. Pickers usually carry whatever they have for sale in the back of a station wagon or truck. They knock on doors, attend farm sales and flea markets—and read classified ads.

For a picker to be successful, he must have a handful of collectors and dealers who are regular customers. Each of these customers must be certain that they receive the first telephone call whenever the picker finds something. Typically, he has each of them convinced he is out there searching for no one else!

Our friend quickly became a successful picker. He found pieces of furniture, stoneware, lamps, coverlets, and folk art in central and western Illinois that amazed us. Over the years, we had operated under the illusion that it was necessary to travel to Ohio, Pennsylvania, New York, and New England to find American country antiques. He was finding great things within an hour of our home.

Recently there was an article in a national antiques publication extolling the virtues of an annual community sale in Paxton, Illinois. Collectors travel to Paxton from throughout middle America to bid on the antiques that turn up at the numerous auctions taking place all over town on a designated day. The collectors who have written the book you are currently struggling through live 45 minutes from Paxton and had never heard of the reknowned community

sale until the article appeared in the magazine.

It is worthwhile to keep abreast of the ever-changing merchandise of local antiques dealers. Regardless of the quality of goods a dealer may stock, at some point something worthwhile is going to make its way into the shop. By assuming a shop was not "up to our standards," we have missed some exceptional buys.

As we noted above, the mission of the successful picker is to buy a particular piece at a reasonable or bargain price, find a buyer, cash the check, continue the hunt, and fill up the truck.

The most successful pickers and antiques dealers are those who would rather sell than collect. If an individual is a dealer/collector, it sometimes creates a conflict of interest: he has a hard time deciding to sell the "best" pieces because he wants them himself.

One of our favorite dealers has a shop filled with significant pieces of American painted furniture, stoneware, and baskets and a house filled with Ethan Allen early American furniture with nutmeg maple stain. His customers know that whenever he buys something it is going to be for sale. He doesn't keep the best example for his own collection and put the "other" one in his shop.

The key to finding country antiques at affordable prices is to be aware of the potential resources in your own immediate geographic area. Try to find out the names of local pickers, schedule regular visits to area shops, seek out individuals who have been serious collectors over the years and may be interested in disposing of some things, communicate with other collectors to let them know what you are seeking, and purchase the next edition of this book. Our youngest son's orthodontist would appreciate it.

A Brief Look at Prices

Recently, while going through a stack of antiques and collectibles magazines stored in a box in the attic, we found a December 1968, issue of *Spinning Wheel*. A monthly publication, *Spinning Wheel* contained a cross-section of articles dealing with all phases of antiques collecting.

On page 4 was an advertisement from The 1670 Tavern Antiques shop in East Haverhill, Massachusetts. The 1670 Tavern had great ads that accurately described the items for sale and did a large mail-order business. In December of 1968 there were eleven pieces that we wish we had purchased for a total of $181.50 (plus postage). They included the following:

Wooden kitchen spoon, 12" long, knob end, $2.50

Unusual dairy table paddle, round handle, $4

All-wood old-fashioned hinged lemon squeezer, $10

Staved sugar firkin or bucket, copper tacks, $12.50

Crudely carved cookie board, sailing ship, $22.50

Lap coffee grinder, top crank, brass hopper, $17.50

Wood edged slate, 13" × 9", dovetailed corners, $4

Rather plain stoneware, blue leaf and stem, $6

Deep big 13" pewter charger, mended but good, $37.50

Adjustable trammal, 31" closed, lug pole hook, $20

Pair of hand-wrought andirons, 13", front loops, $45

Even considering the major changes in the value of the dollar and cost of living increases, the eleven items were incredibly inexpensive in 1968. The staved sugar firkin for $12.50 is worth a minimum of ten times that figure today. If it were painted a strong shade of blue or yellow, it would cost you closer to $300 than $200.

If you want to get violently ill, let us take you back to several 1670 Tavern advertisements from the late 1950s:

January, 1957

Tiny butter mold, cow head design, $5

Swan design butter mold, has metal band, $3.50

17th-century wooden fish from weathervane, $26

Flat bottomed, roundish splint basket, 18", $2.50

Fine 40" butter scales, no paint, $45

Complete walnut spool cabinet, five drawers, $15

February, 1957

Baby's rattle of tin, drum shape, whistle, $2

Rum swiggler, 5" diameter, four iron bands, old blue paint, $5

March, 1957

Marked iron porringer, 5½" by Kendrick, $7.50

Wooden butter stamp with sheep design, $9

E G Booz's Old Cabin Whiskey bottle, blue, $12.50

April, 1957

Tin candle mold, four tube, trays at both ends, $4.50

Round eagle butter stamp, nicely carved, $10

Wooden cookie roller with fish, fern, rabbit, $6

1702 Pennsylvania Dutch decorated
   smoothing board, $40

May, 1957

Stout splint cheese basket, handled,
   25″ diameter, $5
Wood butter stamp, cow design,
   long handle, $6
Red and blue homespun coverlet,
   90″ × 99″, $25

December, 1958

Eagle pattern blue and white homespun coverlet, $15
Hired man's bed, square posts with
   knobs, $12.50
Early unusual high chair, blue, rush
   seat, $17.50
Wood butter stamp, geometric leaf
   design, $1.50
8″ heavy wood plate or trencher,
   $12.50
Fancy cookie mold board, cat and
   dog, two-sided, $18
Brass skimmer, 6″, hand wrought,
   15″ handle, $19

Are you green with envy yet? Thir-
ty years from now, relatives of yours
are going to pick up this volume at
your tag sale and thumb through the
pages. They are going to speculate
about the prices in the book and re-
mark how incredibly inexpensive
items were in the late 1980s—and
how nuts you were not to buy more.

American iron, pewter, and wood-
en ware are difficult to secure today.
In the 1950s there was not a significant demand for imported wooden
ware and iron hearth and cooking
utensils. Collectors could correctly assume that their purchases were
American. As the demand for early
pieces grew in the 1970s and 1980s,
the amount of imported items grew
proportionately.

American cast iron is probably a

reasonably good buy today when you
consider how difficult it is to obtain.

The first furnace that cast iron into
household utensils was established in
Saugus, Massachusetts, in the 1640s.
Cast iron contains a much higher per-
centage of carbon than wrought iron
that is flattened, rather than cast in a
mold.

There was very little wrought iron
made after the 1840s and relatively
few American pieces are offered for
sale. Cast iron was produced from the
middle of the nineteenth century
through the first quarter of the twentieth century. Among the items of cast
iron that still can be found are:

   waffle irons
   trivets
   griddles
   kettles
   mortars and pestles
   skillets
   match safes
   boot jacks
   windmill weights
   apple parers
   "sad" irons
   fluting irons

The majority of imported ironware
available at local shows and shops today is imported from Spain, eastern
Europe, or Mexico. Even factory-
made wooden kitchen implements
like butter paddles, bowls, and spoons
that were mass-produced in huge
quantities from the 1870s through
the 1920s are becoming much more
difficult to locate.

We met an elderly man in New
York state several years ago: his family had owned a wooden ware factory.
When the factory closed in the 1930s,
there were thousands of "blank" butter paddles that had been roughed
out by machine and were ready to be

finished by hand. There were piles of butter paddles and barrels filled with butter paddles. The gentleman used the pieces of maple as kindling for nightly fires over the years, until he decided to put a sack of the few remaining examples aside for his grandchildren.

The demand for quality American antiques will continue to escalate as new collectors begin to understand what is good and what is not. The bargains that will be found probably will be turned up in unlikely places by individuals who had the foresight to search.

1
Country Furniture

Historically, country furniture and folk art have gone from houses, barns, attics, and antiques shops in New England, New York, and Pennsylvania to collectors throughout the United States. Recently, there has been a reverse migration: now pieces of country furniture from the Midwest and Southeast are offered at Eastern antiques shows. As the demand for country furniture increases, pieces that were considered too "rough" a year or two ago will increase in value.

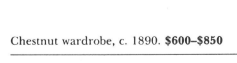

Chestnut wardrobe, c. 1890. **$600–$850**

Shaker Furniture

With the incredible rise in prices for Shaker furniture, there has been a comparable increase in the quantity of pieces marked "Shaker" at shows and auctions. Keep in mind that there were 6000 Shakers in the mid-nineteenth century; by 1900, that number had decreased to 600. The only pieces that the Shakers sold to "the world" were chairs and footstools. As the various communities closed, the Shaker brothers and sisters took their furniture with them to surviving communities. After 1860, there was little furniture constructed for their own use.

If you are going to purchase a piece of Shaker furniture other than a production rocking chair, it is critical to know its provenance (history). The dealer should be able to give some type of documentation about its Shaker origins. There are hundreds of pieces labeled "Shaker" merely because they have the "look."

Painted Furniture

Country collectors tend to assume that painted furniture must be made of a soft wood (pine or poplar) or walnut. There is a wealth of handcrafted painted furniture in Virginia, North Carolina, and South Carolina made of oak.

The task of determining how much work has been done to a particular piece of furniture is more complex for collectors of painted furniture. A multitude of sins can be covered by paint. If a chair has been "pieced out" or height has been added to each leg, paint covers the additions. It is almost impossible to hide repair work or alterations when furniture is refinished.

A painted finish can be described as original, early, or late. If you are going to buy it, you should have some appreciation of what each term means:

original: The first and only coat of paint.

early: Put on the piece at some point after the original paint. The finish is "old" and could be 75 or 150 years old.

late: Normally, a "late" surface is the third or fourth coat of paint, not very old. It could be a few months or 20 years old. On an eighteenth-century cupboard, "late" paint could have been applied in 1870.

In today's market, a painted finish adds much to the value of a piece of furniture. Blue, yellow, and bittersweet are especially popular colors. A cupboard with a white finish can be worth $1000. An identical cupboard with blue paint could be worth $2500. Close inspection of any painted surface is a wise move.

Helpful Hints

1. An unwritten (until now) rule of thumb among collectors is that the best time to purchase a large cupboard at an antiques show is on Sunday afternoon, fifteen minutes before the dealers begin to pack up and go home. The problem with this strategy is that the cupboard you saw on Friday morning when the show opened occasionally will be sold by Sunday. If it hasn't sold, the dealer may be tired of looking at it after three days and give you a more desirable price.
2. Don't tell anyone else, but there are still some rare bargains in country furniture in North and South Carolina.

3. A gentleman who provided us with a great deal of insight about country furniture in the 1960s continues to state that "There is one great treasure in every shop. As you travel down the highway and see a sign for an antiques shop, you must stop because there is a bargain." He's wrong.

Kitchen cupboard, factory made, early 1900s, refinished. **$625–$700**

Two-piece pine kitchen cupboard, c. 1890–1900. **$800–$1000**

Painted pine storage cupboard, Midwestern, mid-nineteenth century. **$475–$575**

Factory-made storage cupboard, walnut, glass front with tin sides, late nineteenth century. **$500–$575**

Painted pie safe, screen wire inserts rather than tin, late nineteenth century, pine, "as found" condition. **$395–$425**

Factory-made kitchen cupboard, maple, "as found" finish, early twentieth century. **$450–$575**

Walnut kitchen cabinet, unusual form, c. 1880, refinished. **$1200–$1500**

Painted pine storage cupboard, bracket base, c. 1860s. **$500–$600**

Chimney cupboard, dark blue paint, 56" high, mid-nineteenth century. **$750–$900**

Pine step-back cupboard, painted finish, c. 1840. **$1600–$2200**

Painted pine pie safe, screen wire inserts in doors, c. 1880. **$500–$575**

Painted pine cupboard, c. 1840s, bracket base. **$750–$900**

Pine cupboard, painted finish, "bootjack" ends, found in North Carolina, c. 1850–1870. **$500–$625**

Crude pine cupboard, painted finish, c. 1870. **$300–$350**

Poplar "jelly" or "jam" cupboard, factory made, late nineteenth century. **$400–$475**

Handcrafted kitchen cupboard, mid-nineteenth century, pine. **$475–$575**

Pine step-back cupboard, c. 1860s, painted finish. **$1800–$2200**

Pine step-back cupboard, "open" form, painted finish, mid-nineteenth century. **$850–$1200**

Factory-made cupboard, oak and poplar, early 1900s. **$400–$500**

Factory-made pie safe, painted finish, c. 1880, walnut and poplar. **$300–$400** as is; **$500–$585** refinished

Early pine storage cupboard with paneled doors, "rough" condition, c. 1840. **$375–$450** as is; **$550–$600** refinished

Pine pie safe, "late" painted finish, six pierced tin panels in doors, late nineteenth century. **$425–$555**

Painted pine pie safe, hand-pierced tins, possibly Pennsylvania in origin, c. 1870s. **$450–$525**

Partially stripped pine pie safe, c. 1880.
$375–$400 as is; **$500–$575** stripped;
$800–$1100 old blue paint

Pine storage cupboard with pierced tin sides, probably Midwestern in origin, painted finish, c. 1860. **$600–$685**

Walnut pie safe, c. 1875. **$55**

Factory-made kitchen cabinet, refinished, early 1900s. **$575–$650**

Painted pine pie safe, elaborately pierced tins, probably Pennsylvania in origin, c. 1840s. **$1200–$1600**

Pine pie safe, "as found" condition, c. 1880. **$300–$375** as is; **$500–$575** refinished

Factory-made kitchen cabinet, maple and pine, early 1900s. **$600–$685**

Painted pine storage cupboard, handcrafted, c. 1850s. **$400–$450**

Factory-made oak and ash icebox, original hardware, c. 1900, refinished. **$475–$575**

Factory-made cupboard, maple and poplar, early 1900s. **$500–$575**

Pine cupboard, early 1900s, refinished. **$300–$375**

Exceptional pie safe, hand-pierced tins, painted finish, c. 1840s. **$850–$1200**

Refinished "jam" or "jelly" cupboard, pine and poplar, Midwestern in origin, c. 1875. **$450–$550**

Maple storage cabinet, c. 1870, refinished. **$850–$1200**

Poplar and pine pie safe, c. 1880, refinished. **$600-$750**

Factory-made kitchen cabinet, original hardware, c. 1900, refinished. **$450–$525**

Walnut pie safe, mid-nineteenth century. **$500–$585**

Factory-made kitchen cabinet, maple and pine, c. 1900, refinished. **$675–$700**

"Blind front" pine cupboard, late nineteenth century, refinished. **$750–$850**

Factory-made kitchen cabinet, c. 1920, refinished. **$400–$475**

Pine storage cupboard, unusual form, c. 1875. **$350–$425**

Factory-made cupboard, c. 1920.
$385–$450

Half-spindle-back chair, pine and maple,
c. 1880, refinished. **$65–$85**

Pressed-back oak chairs, factory made, c.
1900, refinished. **$800–$1200**, set of four.
Round oak table with claw feet.
$750–$950

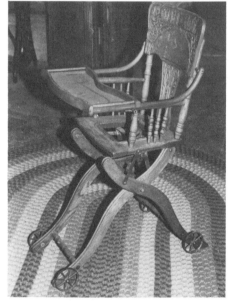

Oak child's highchair, iron wheels,
"pressed" decoration, c. 1890, refinished.
$250–$275

Pine child's chair, splint seat, splayed legs, late nineteenth century. **$75–$90**

Factory-made highchair, maple and pine, painted finish, c. 1880. **$100–$125**

Stripped pine bench, found in Illinois, 18″ high, 22″ long, early twentieth century. **$85–$125**

Shaker community footstool, not made for commercial sale, painted green, c. 1870. **$250–$350**

Child's table and chair set, c. 1940. **$150–$200**

Windsor settle, original painted and decorated finish, New England, c. 1830. **$4500–$5500**

Arrow-back mammy's bench, pine, hickory, and maple, c. 1860, refinished. **$475–$575**

Adirondack chair, splint seating, factory made, c. 1900. **$300–$375**

Pine bench, painted finish, early twentieth century. **$325–$400**

Splayed leg bench, painted finish, "as found" condition, early 1900s. **$55–$65**

Unusual pie safe from North Carolina. **$400–$475**

Country store coffee bin. **$400–$485**

Granite ware pan. **$65–$75**

Red sugar bucket. **$225–$275**

Stoneware jug with slip-cup decoration. **$135–$150**

Three-gallon stoneware jar. **$175–$225**

Commercial sign doubles as broom holder. **$350–$425**

Family of old teddy bears. **$400–$500**

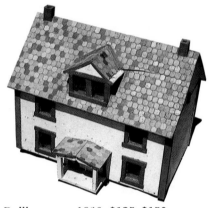

Dollhouse, c. 1930. **$125–$150**

Adirondack chair, early 1900s. **$175– $200**

Painted pine desk, c. 1870. **$325–$375**

Cast-iron windmill weight. **$575–$625**

Painted pine doll cradle. **$55–$70**

Field basket, **$225–$275**; painted child's bed, **$300–$350**.

Dry sink from New York state, c. 1880. **$500–$600**

Pine pie safe, c. 1860s. **$425–$500**

Reproduction child's highchair, yellow worn paint, splint seat, c. 1987. **$150–$175**

Pine spring wagon seat, c. 1915, refinished. **$175–$200**

Twig arm chairs, unfinished, c. 1987. **$100–$120** each

Child's ladder-back rocking chair, worn paint, "as found" condition, c. 1850. **$65–$85**

Oak child's rocking chair, replaced seat, painted finish, c. 1900. **$95–$125**

Painted ladder-back chair, splint seat, mid-nineteenth century. **$150–$175**

Handmade ladder-back chair, maple and pine, "flame" finials, painted finish, c. 1850. **$150–$175**

Cast iron and maple school desk, c. 1920, repainted. **$50–$60**

Factory-made kitchen chair, pine and maple, painted finish, half-spindle form, late nineteenth century. **$75–$100** each

Child's ladder-back rocking chair, c. 1900, refinished. **$60–$75**

New England splayed-leg stool, maple and pine, early nineteenth century, refinished. **$200–$225**

Pine bench, painted and worn finish, mortised base, late nineteenth century. **$135–$150**

Farm or dining table, pine with turned maple legs, c. 1870. **$550–$650**

Press-back armchair, cane seat, oak, c. 1890, refinished. **$225–$250**

Oak bolt cabinet from hardware store, factory made, c. 1890. **$1200–$1500**

Bentwood swivel chair, oak and maple, cane seat, c. 1900, refinished. **$300–$350**

Child's table and press-back chairs, early twentieth century, refinished. **$150–$200,** table; **$420–$500,** 6 chairs

Carpenter's storage chest, dovetailed, pine, c. 1890. **$325–$385**

Collection of press-backed oak dining or side chairs, c. 1890–1915. **$150–$200** each

Pine drop-leaf table, painted base with scrubbed top, c. 1860s. **$400–$500**

Lift-top counter desk, pine, c. 1885. **$125–$150**

Dome top trunk, pine, dovetailed construction, painted finish, c. 1850. **$225–$275**

Painted storage cupboard, pine, Midwestern, c. 1870s. **$350–$400**

Smoking stand, Adirondack style, c. 1900. **$100–$125**

Refinished pine trunk, iron bands, late nineteenth century. **$200–$285**

Immigrant's chest, dome top, painted, mid-nineteenth century. **$325–$385**

Pine storage chest, 40″ x 22″ deep, painted, c. 1915. **$185–$225**

Refinished pine cradle, dovetailed, c. 1850. **$175–$225**

Chest of drawers, pine, painted, c. 1850. **$550–$675**

Refinished pine dry sink, found in Michigan, c. 1875. **$425–$550**

Pine harvest table, painted base with a scrubbed top, c. 1860s. **$750–$1000**

Pine base of a cupboard, painted finish, c. 1840. **$325–$395**

Wood box made from a grocery store coffee bin, painted, "as found" condition, c. 1900. **$95–$120**

Painted blanket chest, bracket base, c. 1830. **$550–$650**

Painted blanket box, pine, c. 1860. **$300–$375**

Factory-made bedside table, "as found" condition, c. 1900. **$75–$85**

Scrub-top pine dining table, painted base, c. 1840. **$675–$850**

Refinished chest, ash and pine, c. 1900.
$150–$200

Refinished sugar chest, dovetailed, pine,
chest-on-frame construction, c. 1840.
$375–$500

Painted sugar chest, mid-nineteenth century. **$600–$800**

Unusual painted cradle, c. 1880.
$300–$375

Large pine desk with turned legs, lift lid,
painted. **$450–$575**

Bracket base blanket chest, pine, painted,
New England, c. 1820. **$1200–$1500**

Grain painted chest of drawers, bracket base, c. 1850. **$500–$600**

Refinished "jam" or "jelly" cupboard, c. 1860. **$350–$425**

Maple meat block, factory made, early 1900s, refinished. **$300–$350**

Factory-made trunk, early 1900s, refinished. **$225–$275**

Refinished pine dry sink, c. 1890. **$425–$550**

Reproduction wood box, made from old wood, total lack of wear, painted finish. **$50–$75**

Painted dry sink, pine, c. 1860. **$1000–$1250**

Pine settle bench, probably English in origin, mid-nineteenth century, refinished. **$550–$700**

Pine table, painted finish, mid-nineteenth century. **$300–$350**

Oak chest of drawers, factory made, c. 1920. **$275–$300**

34

Pine bucket bench, painted and worn finish, early 1900s. **$100–$150**

Immigrant's chest, pine, dovetailed construction, c. 1840, refinished. **$285–$400**

Child's rope bed, "as found" condition, c. 1870. **$250–$300**

Zinc-lined milk cooler, painted and stencilled decoration, excellent original condition, c. 1900. **$1000–$1200**

Storage bin, pine and poplar, late nineteenth century. **$275–$350**

Pine dough box, "bootjack" ends, painted, late nineteenth century. **$275–$325**

Small sawbuck table, pine, twentieth century, refinished. **$200–$225**

Six-board blanket chest, painted finish, turned legs, c. 1850. **$300–$375**

Refinished pine dry sink, c. 1880. **$450–$500**

Walnut "map" case, factory made, early 1900s. **$350–$400**

Unusually small chest of drawers, "old" finish, c. 1830. **$400–$550**

Pine and poplar cupboard, c. 1870s, refinished. **$450–$495**

Six-drawer spool chest from a country store, c. 1880. **$500–$575**

Pine storage chest from an Illinois animal hospital, c. 1900. **$350–$450**

Refinished pine cupboard, step-back with a "glazed" front, mid-nineteenth century. **$1250–$1500**

Refinished blanket box, pine, dovetailed construction, c. 1880. **$300–$350**

Child's cupboard, late nineteenth century, refinished. **$450–$525**

Collection of rope beds from the mid-nineteenth century. **$400–$550** each

2
Southern Country Antiques

This chapter was prepared by Bruce Lube. He is a recognized authority on furniture restoration and an active collector who also writes articles for *Antique Week* and *Carolina Antiques News*.

Virginia, Kentucky, Tennessee, North and South Carolina, and Georgia are usually included in the definition of "Southern" for antiques purposes. For the most part, territory east of the Appalachian Mountains and from Virginia southward falls into the defined region. While it might be argued that additional states should be added to this region, the rationale is that this was the territory undergoing rapid development during the time period of interest, approximately 1700 to 1900. The population in this area during the eighteenth and nineteenth cen-

A pine six-board blanket box from the Winston-Salem area of North Carolina, c. 1820. Note the remaining original "C" scroll bracket foot on the front. The missing one probably fell victim to a vacuum cleaner. Traces of the original reddish-brown paint are still evident. **$1050**

turies was mostly rural. The isolation of rural life and the existing class structure contributed to the inhabitants' need to create practical items for everyday use—what have now become "country antiques." Other factors that have made this region unique include the abundance of raw materials and specialized cultural and practical lifestyles.

This chapter provides a look at a cross-section of Southern country antiques and presents the results of a 1988 survey of antiques dealers and collectors in the region.

Pottery

Pottery is one of the most typical groups of antiques found. High-quality clay deposits exploited in the first half of the eighteenth century in North Carolina and Northern Georgia permitted the high-temperature firing required to produce stoneware. High temperatures also encouraged the technique of sprinkling salt in the kiln during firing. The end product was the hard, rough-textured, durable pottery often found in this region. The popularity of stoneware stimulated potters to create a variety of shapes for many uses. Included among these were storing salt-cured meat, molasses, milk products, lard, and whiskey. The Catawba Valley and Seagrove, North Carolina, were the centers of production for pottery of this type. Identification when no marks are present requires that you be able to recognize the style of a particular piece, type of clay, firing characteristics, and glazes used.

Textiles

Women of the rural South found sewing to be a necessity of life. They made essentials, such as clothing and quilts, as well as decorative textiles to make their homes more attractive and to demonstrate their skills. They often met for quilting bees, which were social as well as practical gatherings, allowing the women to visit while putting the batting and backing on the pieced top made by the lady of the house.

Quilts were first made as essentials for life in cold, often drafty, cabins; quilters made use of any fabric scraps available. By the mid-1800s, factory-made quilts for everyday use became more obtainable; handmade quilts then became more elaborate and decorative, a personal expression of the seamstress. Designs documented special occurrences, such as births and weddings, and included everyday scenes with such names as Harvest Sun and Flying Geese. Religious themes were also popular, with such patterns as the Tree of Life, Star of Bethlehem, and Forbidden Fruit.

In addition to the quilts that enjoyed the status of family heirlooms, tatting, also known as "poor man's lace," was used to make doilies, table scarves, and other decorative items for the home. The creativity and industriousness of these women produced a vast array of handmade textiles, many of which remain for our enjoyment.

Baskets

The utlitarian baskets made from a variety of locally available materials have become another type of country antique. Split oak, river cane, honeysuckle, twig and vine, bark, pine needles, sweet grass, and palmetto were some of the materials used. Those baskets created by Europeans often combined the styles of their Old World cultures with techniques learned from the American Indian. Africans tended to adhere more closely to the styles of their ancestors. Woven baskets were used for everything from carrying water to hauling trash. As with many homemade crafts, they were produced as a family activity.

For those skilled in the art, with the time and patience needed, baskets were also bartered for goods and services. This practice was typical of the rural community. The art and skills required for basketmaking are still found today and basketry is gaining in popularity in some areas. Baskets made in the middle to late 1800s have come into their own as a collectible, achieving prices that range into the hundreds of dollars. The difficulty arises in finding and dating pre-1900 baskets.

Furniture

Among the most diverse groups of Southern country antiques is furniture. Perhaps no other group of collectibles is so varied, since every home needed essentials and a wide selection of local materials was readily available. The carpentry skills of the man of the house, for instance, had an influence on the quantity and quality of products made, as did the availability of woods. This combination of factors guaranteed that many one-of-a-kind items were produced. Even such common furnishings as tables and chairs display infinite variety.

Other furniture was made for special purposes, some unique to the South. The Southern *huntboard slab*, also referred to as a *sideboard*, is one of those. The term *slab* is indicative of its original construction: a thick piece of slab wood from a tree was used; four holes were drilled at the corners, into which legs were mounted. They were designed for gatherings before and after the hunt. In Virginia especially,

hunting from horseback was popular and standing around the huntboard was more comfortable than sitting. A typical table was about 48 inches tall, so leaning against it was comfortable while eating and drinking buffet style. A single drawer or a pair of drawers were added later and used to hold hunt-related paraphernalia. Huntboards created for the aristocracy by the high skilled craftsmen of the day incorporated Hepplewhite and Sheraton designs.

Albeit a useful item, the huntboard's origin and the fact that it was limited to wealthy households in a narrow region, means that surviving examples are difficult to find. Occasionally, they may be mistaken for examples of the more common sideboards of later years. But authentic examples can be found, and the price usually reflects their rarity (confirmed by a 1988 survey of dealers and collectors who handle country antiques from this region).

Best Finds

The forty-plus dealers and collectors who were surveyed were asked about the "best" locations for finding Southern country antiques: North Carolina and Virginia were the top "vote getters." The rich clay deposits and abundant forests of North Carolina fostered the crafting of a great deal of stoneware and pine furniture. These two states also enjoyed rapid development, as pioneers claimed the lands and moved West and South from the early colonies of Jamestown and Williamsburg.

The dealers and collectors who responded indicated that, while the supply of country antiques is still ample, high-quality items are getting more and more difficult to find.

The examples of Southern pottery, furniture, baskets, and textiles shown on the following pages were gathered from antiques shops and private collections in January, 1988. They are representative of the Southern antiques still being found by collectors.

This 14-inch-tall storage jar is marked "J.D. Craven"; he is a known potter from the Randolph County, North Carolina, area. Excellent condition. **$175**

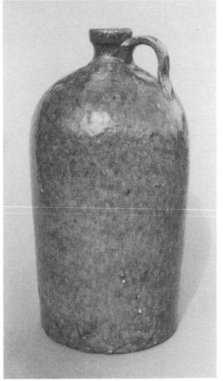

This one-gallon, alkaline glazed jug is unsigned but attributed to a potter named Ritchie from the Catawba Valley in North Carolina. Dated c. 1890. **$120**

Catawba Valley, North Carolina, c. 1890, is the origin of this jug with "X" incised in clay before it was fired. The "X" denotes its use as a container for moonshine and is found near the handle. One-half-gallon capacity, alkaline glaze. **$125**

Stoneware canning jar from North Carolina, c. 1890. **$145**

A red ware dish, c. 1890, 8 inches in diameter, from the Randolph County, North Carolina, area. **$75**

This 4-inch-diameter, brown glazed utility bowl is dated c. 1880 and is from the Randolph County, North Carolina, pottery region. **$195**

North Carolina oak-splint buttocks basket, c. 1890. **$265**

North Carolina "tobacco spit," glazed, double-handled jug, one handle missing. **$130**

This solid cherry piece has several names, including *feed chest*, *sugar box*, and *high blanket box*. The hardware is original but repairs have been made to the lower drawer. By running your hand across its surface you can tell it has been hand planed. Close examination also shows the slight graduation in the size of the drawers, a mark of craftsmanship; c. 1810, probably of Pennsylvania origin. **$1800**

This pine milk cupboard was made in Cabarrus County, North Carolina, c. 1810. It has hand-wrought rose-head nails, forged hinges, bracket feet, one-board sides, and hand-planed plank door; some of the original red paint is still visible. **$800**

Cherry bonnet chest with original Sandwich glass pulls and tiger maple inlays above pineapple-cut columns. Note the smaller second drawer, with subsequent drawers increasing in size, denoting craftsmanship in its construction. Chest was made c. 1880. **$785**

A striking example of the Sheraton style, this c. 1830–1850 walnut candlestand is extremely sturdy. **$375**

A black cabinetmaker from Morganton, North Carolina, made this pine plantation desk, c. 1840–1860. Although this piece was unsigned, the maker was known to have signed some items. **$750**

An impressive 8-foot, 4-inch, walnut corner cabinet. The cabinet was traced through wills filed in the Mecklenburg County, North Carolina, courthouse to its origin between 1820 and 1835. The pulls have been replaced but otherwise it is all original. Pegged construction, lower doors have chamfered panels on the inside, two-board back. Note that the sides go straight back, which is typical of southern cabinets, while in the North the sides often flare out. An outstanding piece. **$7900**

North Carolina Cherokee Indian basket, c. 1890–1900. It is difficult to find and date baskets earlier than this. **$185**

Pine work table, c. 1865, from an estate in York County, South Carolina. It has a three-board tongue and groove top, mortise and tenon legs that are pegged, and red paint showing under the flaky white. The table is 27 inches high. **$190**

Pine huntboard from Clio, South Carolina, c. 1850. The top is pegged to the base and the legs are mortised and pegged into the sides. The piece measures 53 inches long and is 41 inches tall. **$4800**

Blue and white are the predominant colors in this Irish Chain quilt, influenced by the Ocean Waves pattern. It was made in the late 1800s in Rowan County, North Carolina, by a skilled quilter. **$300**

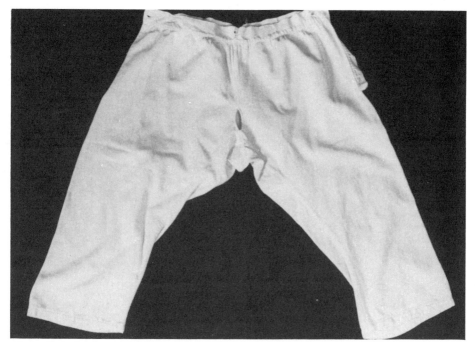

These little boy's trousers provided a strategically located cutout. The trousers came from an estate in Old Salem, North Carolina. **$20**

An oak-splint berry basket from the Southern Appalachian region, probably Tennessee, c. 1910. **$50**

Applied tulip pattern quilt, made c. 1850 in Davidson County, North Carolina. The stitching shows Pennsylvania Dutch influence. The mustard orange, blue, and green used are typical of the vegetable dyes during that time. **$250**

3
Kitchen and Hearth Antiques

This chapter was prepared by Teri and Joe Dziadul, and illustrates items from their extensive collection. The Dziaduls have been filling specific requests for more than 20 years, and offer a lengthy list of kitchen and hearth antiques to collectors and dealers. The current list may be obtained by sending $1 to 6 South George Washington Road, Enfield, CT 06082.

People have become fascinated not only by the history of cookery, but by the implements connected with it. Gourmet cookery had its start in the early kitchen. Herbs such as sage, sweet marjoram, savory and thyme dried in the tin kitchen and hung in the fireplace cupboard. Antique kitchen utensils with their great functional beauty have, logically, become an important field for collectors.

Our ancestors prepared their foods in heavy black iron pots for more than 200 years. The swinging crane and the bubbling pot yielded many succulent

Cast-iron bowl; c. 1875. **$75–$95**

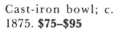

meals. A boiled dinner could be counted upon to keep a man putting up a stone wall, well-fueled until his evening meal. On the hearth stood the Dutch oven, a broad kettle with long legs, and a lid turned up all around the rim. Bread dough and biscuits were baked here, a pile of hot coals on the hearth and more coals heaped onto the lid to provide top and bottom heat. Iron implements used in the embers were called "down hearth" utensils. Skillets or spiders were thrust into the hot coals of maple for cooking griddlecakes and frying venison. Perhaps the most beautiful pieces of hearth equipment were the toasters. Hand wrought, their designs are unique and delicate. They toasted bread and possibly cheese. Life centered about the hearth, principal source of warmth, nourishment, and cheer.

By the 1870s, a Colonial wife would have regarded the Yankee kitchen as a place of modern marvels. The heavy iron pots of fireplace and down hearth cookery had been replaced by lighter ware of coated steel. The housewife of that day, in a full-gathered gingham apron tied over a many-gored skirt, shot a dollop of kerosene onto the crumpled pages of the *Boston Transcript*, as Kenneth Roberts has related, and put six sticks of kindling and three of stovewood into the firebox; she was ready to make toast, boil the coffee, and coddle the eggs. Soon enticing aromas mingled with the smell of geranium leaves.

At the table, wooden trenchers (plates) were piled high with smoking meat — hashes, thick stews, venison — and pumpkin sauce or pie for dessert. Trenchers were often used for two courses, simply by turning them over. Upcountry they spoke of the "dinner side and the pie side." The Colonists' turning mill produced *treen* (made of tree) bowls, plates, funnels, butter stamps, and other small useful objects. The use of wooden tableware continued in rural areas until the late 1800s.

Muffin pans, long-handled spoons, pie-crimpers, choppers, apple parers, and coffee grinders were still familiar sights. A pantry held a brilliant array of jewel-toned jellies, homemade relishes, pickled peaches with the pointed ears of cloves dotting their amber sides.

At every economic level, conveniences were lacking in all phases of domestic routine. Lighting an entire room was not a common performance. Wealthy families used as many as seven large candles in a room, but in ordinary households, a single candle was lit to illuminate a book page or a section of needlework.

Acquiring antiques and collectibles for the kitchen and hearth is, for some, an art. For many others, it is a hobby that should be fun and long-lasting. It requires patience, a trained eye, and knowledge. One must be ever alert to the possibility of purchasing a newly made fake. We are all familiar with the occasional museum acquisition mistakes by acknowledged experts. When an object has tremendous popular appeal, it will more often that not appeal to the forger as well. If you specialize, you will become familiar with the standards for the objects in your interest area and, thus, less susceptible to fakes and forgeries.

Tilter tea kettle; iron, early 18th century; arm extends over spout by which the kettle was tilted when water was needed. Hook hangs on crane. **$425–$495**

Iron dutch oven; early 19th century; hot ashes heaped under pot and on the lid so that even bread could be baked inside. **$295–$375**

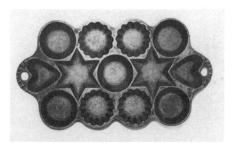

Cast-iron muffin pan; marked "Reid's Pan, Dec. 1870." **$195–$250**

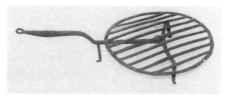

Wrought iron gridiron; 18th century, revolving stand, used to broil meat or fish. **$225–$275**

Wrought iron bread toaster; 18th century; has feet for sitting before the fire, revolving head turns the bread for toasting on both sides. **$275–$325**

Tin apple roasters; c. 1850; placed in front of the fire, curved shelves hold sizzling juices. **$450–$525**

Footwarmers; necessary in unheated churches. Samuel Sewall, on a chill Sunday, wrote in his diary: "This day so cold that the sacramental bread is frozen pretty hard and rattles sadly." Pierced tin box in wood frame, receptacle inside holds hot coals. Used in sleighs and buggies in cold weather, c. 1850, **$275–$295**. Pierced sunburst design, signed I. Hotchkis, c. 1840, **$295–$350**.

Toddy Warmer; thrust into hot coals to warm drink, c. 1840. **$275–$295**

Cast-iron coffee bean roaster; three legs, set into stove hole opening, wire basket, c. 1880. **$285–$345**

Biscuit stamps and prickers; wood with iron prongs; early 19th century. An early trade journal, c. 1804, states that the moulder forms two biscuits at a time; the maker stamps and passes them to the splitter who separates them, etc. Sheaf of Wheat, **$275–$295**; Princess Royal, **$350–$395**.

Cast-iron Minuteman andirons; rare subject, mid-19th century. Collection of Martha Dziadul Doak. **$600–$725**

Flour sifter and wood tazza. Wood sifter, c. 1861, with original paper label, **$295–$325**; wood tazza, turned stem, early nails, c. 1870, **$195–$235**.

Crimping board; wooden board and roller (acorn finials) for gathering and pleating ruffles, c. 1800. **$250–$295**

54

Spice cabinets. Wood, porcelain labels and knobs, c. 1890, **$275–$295**; wood, pewter scroll labels, bottom drawer labelled Nutmeg Grater, **$295–$325**.

Wood goblet and open salt; goblet turned from one piece of wood, c. 1870, **$95–$110**; footed salt, **$75–$95**.

Miniature treen items; late 19th century. Mortar and pestle, **$50–$60**. Rare caster set, **$195–$225**. Kettle, three-legged, wire handle, **$125–$145**. Bucket, staved, tin bands, **$85–$95**. Salt-box, hinged lid, **$125–$145**. Piggin, staved, tin bands, Wm. S. Tower, So. Hingham, Mass., **$95–$125**.

Lemon reamers. Wood, corrugated head with turned handle, c. 1875, **$175–$195**. Glass, marked "Little Handy Lemon Squeezer, Silver and Co., New York," **$95–$110**. Wood, satiny patina, c. 1860, **$195–$225**.

Butter Stamps. Lollypop, chamfered handle, c. 1800, **$425–$450**. Double-ended stamp from one piece of wood, flower stamp on one, butter worker on other, **$375–$425**. Radial disk, six-lobed geometric design, c. 1840, **$165–$185**. Butter roller, c. 1875, carved cow, used on oblong pound of butter. Scarce cow roller design. **$325–$375**. Half-round print, sheaf of wheat carving, c. 1850, this version never had a handle, **$275–$295**.

Butter stamps and molds. Simply carved fruit, probably an apple, **$110–$125**. Case mold, peach, **$175–$195**. Case mold, swan, **$145–$175**.

Wooden sugar bowls; bail handles; mid-19th century. **$395–$895**

Butter prints. Very deeply carved eagle, c. 1850, **$495–$550**. Stylized flower and leaves, c. 1870, **$95–$110**. Wading bird, stork, c. 1860, **$700–$750**. Flowers in basket, c. 1870, **$350–$395**

Kitchen utensils. Wood funnel, turned with chamfered spout, c. 1875, **$150–$165**. Hamlinite potato peeler, tin with grit surface, c. 1920, **$45–$55**. Pot lid lifter, wood handle, wrought iron hook, c. 1880, **$95–$125**. Everett raisin seeder, wood and wire, c. 1890, **$50–$65**.

Lemon knives, c. 1860–1890. EPNS engraved blades, wood carved handles, **$165–$185**.

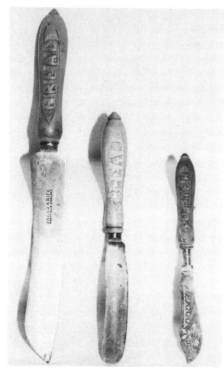

Bread and butter knives, c. 1860–1890. Steel blade, carved wood handle, **$65–$75**. Carved wood handle, to accompany small breadboard, **$85–$95**. EPNS engraved blade, carving on wood handle, **$65–$75**.

Butter molds, c. 1880. Heart, very deep carving, **$425–$475**. Hen, rare subject, **$475–$495**. Fish, detailed carving, **$450–$495**.

Carved wood bread boards, c. 1870. "Our Daily Bread," **$165–$195**. "Bread," **$55–$75**. "Staff of Life," **$165–$195**.

Half-round butter prints, c. 1860. Very deep carving, pineapple design, **$425–$495**. Thistle, friction fit handle, **$425–$495**. Vigilant cow, rare, **$650–$695**.

Large cutting board, tombstone shape, hanging hole at top. **$85–$95**

Bakery sign, 18½″ long, 19th century baker's trade symbol, original gold leaf. **$625–$695**

Wood apple peeler. Built on a board, the cog wheels and belts were devised to turn the arm that held the apple. These wooden parers were used in the late 18th and early 19th centuries until the patented iron corers took their place. This piece has many Shaker characteristics. **$425–$495**

Painted pantry boxes. The smaller sizes held sugar, spices, and meal. Old boxes are being newly painted, and the value is greatly diminished. Mustard yellow, black cover, **$275–$300**; dark green, pointed lap fingers, **$275–$300**.

Tenth anniversary tin, men's rubbers. Gifts ranged in size from miniature to immense, c. 1880. **$525–$595**

Woven tin in the manner of splint baskets. Traces of green paint. For table decoration, this was a practical gift, c. 1870, **$550–$595**. Tin wall pocket with three sections, **$475–$495**.

Wood apple parer; Shaker, clamps to table. **$525–$575**

Tenth anniversary tin. Tin whimsies were presented to couples at celebration parties. The novelties very often provided the evening's entertainment. Rare punch decorated oversized tin rattle, inscribed "December 8, 1879, For Boys Only." For a couple with no daughters? **$1,200–$1,400**

Tin flour sifter, marked "Earnshaw's Patent, July 25, 1866." All tin, revolving blades sift flour over wire screen. **$125–$145**

Wood noggins, made from a single block of wood. Some have rounded or chamfered sides. They held rum and ale at first, and then cider when orchards began to thrive. Late 18th and early 19th centuries. **$125–$375**

Pair of tin whimsey men's slippers with painted red and black bows, one of the few known painted pieces of anniversary tin, c. 1850. **$1,000–$1,100**.

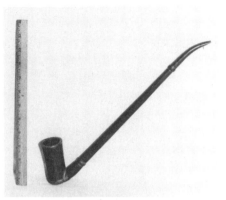

Tin whimsey church warden's pipe, c. 1850. The bowl is double walled. **$1,000–$1,100**

Tin spice cannisters and carrier. Lids have incised spice titles, c. 1870. **$600–$700**. Tin whimsey goblet, fashioned from a funnel, ice cream spoons, and a maple sugar mold, c. 1870. **$450–$495**.

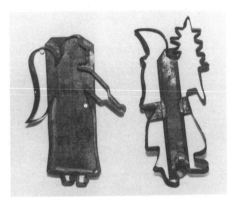

Tin cookie cutters, Nineteenth century angel, 8 inches, **$325–$395**. Nineteenth century Father Christmas with tree, 8 inches, **$400–$450**.

Heart in Hand tin cookie cutter; a rare and desirable motif. The outline of a 3-year-old child's hand was often traced since his heart was still pure. **$650–$700**

Tin cookie cutters. Rabbit, **$75–$85**; woman with defined bosom, **$300–$395**; bird, **$65–$75**.

Tin cookie cutters; a man and woman in early attire, the pair. **$225–$250**

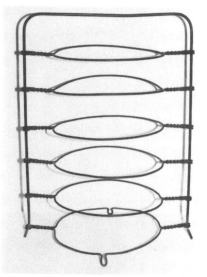

Wire pie rack for holding a stack of six pies for cooling and storage. **$75–$85**

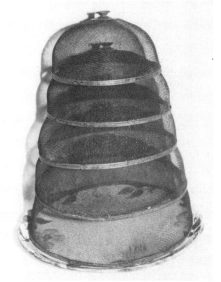

Nest of five fly screen covers, placed over plate of food. Marked "Johnson's Improved Dish Cover–Pat. Pend." In fine condition, the nest. **$275–$300**

Ice cream scoop and mold. Tin ice cream scoop, marked "Clewell's Pat. Nov. 17, 1878," V Clad Maker, **$45–$55**; pewter ice cream mold, bust of Washington, **$55–$65**.

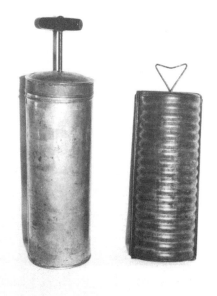

Syllabub churn and brown bread mold. Tin cylinder churn with a perforated dasher to whip up a high, frothy mixture. "Pat. Sept. 14, '75," **$80–$90**; tin brown bread mold, uncommon flat back, **$45–$55**.

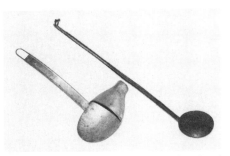

Tin pie crimpers, sometimes given as a practical tenth wedding anniversary gift; 6½" long, 2¼" diameter wheel, **$175–$185**; 9½" long, with hanging end, **$275–$300**.

Tallow pourer and scoop: melted animal fats were skimmed of impurities before they could be used for making candles. A tallow scoop served that purpose. They are made for both left and right hand use. Tin tallow pourer, c. 1860, **$195–$225**; tin tallow scoop, c. 1850, **$225–$250**.

Knee-rest nutcracker; iron, upright truncated bar with a slightly depressed top for cupping the nut as it was struck soundly; early 19th century. **$55–$65**

Food choppers, early 19th century; the variety of chopping knives is fascinating. Never idle, these knives were much used in the preparation of daily meals. Iron chopper, blade 9½" long, wood handle, **$125–$150**; iron blade, 6½" long, wood handle, **$60–$75**.

Red ware dish; made principally during the 18th and 19th centuries. Used for everyday tableware, the design was simple. A liquid clay known as "slip" was very often applied in designs such as splotches, wavy lines, flowers, various names and expressions. This 10"-diameter dish with yellow slipware scrolly decoration and "Hannah" slip-trailed in center. Much of the slip has worn off. Coggled edge. **$700–$800**

Mocha ware. Cream ware pottery, principally made in England between 1780 and 1840. Covered mustard jar, red earthworm decoration on a white ground, striped brown bands, **$275–$325**. Footed salt cellar, blue seaweed on white ground, **$200–$225**. Footed salt cellar, brown seaweed on white ground, **$250–$275**. Mug, brown seaweed on orange background, brown banding, **$250–$295**.

Yellow ware mold. Bird eating from basket of fruit, c. 1890. **$295–$325**

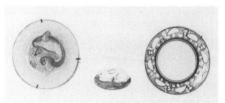

Dedham pottery; from pottery located in Dedham, Massachusetts, around 1895. The body is of gray stoneware with a crackle glaze and cobalt design of birds, animals, and flowers. There are thirteen standard patterns and the rabbit was chosen for the company logo. Other designs were produced for special orders. Dolphin plate, 6″ diameter, **$600–$650**; figural rabbit paperweight, **$450–$475**; mushroom plate, 6″ diameter, **$225–$250**.

Horn lantern, originally spelled *lanthorne*, c. 1750. Cow horn is used for windows. Strap tin ring provides carrying handle or for hanging. Hood ventilators furnish essential draft. **$475–$575**

Old millinery materials are arranged in old containers by Doris Stauble of Wiscasset, Maine. Basket with silk flowers and fruits, **$175–$195**; painted firkin with cherries and birds, **$250–$295**; painted wood container with glass berries, **$295–$325**.

Covered copper saucepans, late 19th century: 8″ in diameter, "D.H. & M. Co. Wooster St., N.Y.," **$250–$275**; 10″ in diameter, marked as above, **$275–$300**.

Stoneware preserve jars: A. Conrad & Co., New Geneva, Pennsylvania, jar, **$250–$275**; Lyons, NY, covered crock, **$250–$275**; unmarked Pennsylvania jar, **$150–$175**.

Kettle lamp, wrought iron, early 19th century. Trunnion mounted, the central wick support eliminates the problem of drip. **$450–$495**

A signed basket, made by B. G. Higgins, The Basket Shop, Chesterfield, Massachusetts, 11½" diameter. "Mrs. Eleanor McCarthy" is written in pencil on the rim. The Higgins family made baskets in Massachusetts for several generations and prices are escalating dramatically. **$375–$475**

Butter Churns. Wood-staved construction, old original red paint, **$350–$395**. Gray stoneware, "J. Fisher & Co., Lyons, NY." Cobalt blue tulip design and number 5, **$1,200–$1,400**.

Candle dipper and dryer. These pieces are from a turnstile stand that was used in a candlemaker's shop. It held 400 candles at a time. Each circular dipper could be removed from the turnstile arms, dipped, and then returned to the arm. Without moving himself, the candlemaker rotated the turnstile to the next spoke and repeated the process. Eighteenth-century turnstile candle dipper and dryer with eight pieces, **$2,400–$2,600**. Individual circular dipper and dryer, **$275–$300**.

Stoneware Jugs. Four gallon jug, large cobalt bird on leafy branch, "New York Stoneware Co., Fort Edward, NY," **$850–$950**. Four gallon ovoid jug, cobalt cherries and leaves, "F. H. Cowden, Harrisburg, PA," **$600–$700**.

Tin candle molds: three dozen tubes, with a very unusual interlocking grid secured over the top to hold the wicks in place, **$450–$475**; six-tube mold with typical Pennsylvania base and stretcher, **$295–$325**.

Candy containers: cat, Germany, c. 1900, head lifts off, **$275–$295**; fish, glass eyes, realistic paint colors, **$225–$295**.

Chocolate molds: *top row*, Father Christmas, 6″ high, **$150–$175**; Father Christmas on motorcycle, **$225–$250**. *Bottom row*, miniature Father Christmas, Riecke & Co., **$95–$110**; St. Nicholas with children in tub, Anton Reiche, **$295–$350**; Father Christmas on donkey, **$165–$185**.

Wood frame candle mold, contains eight tin tubes, each with handle, 19th century. **$850–$950**

Tin candle molds: twelve-tube candle mold with strap handle; frame at top and bottom, wire ring for hanging, c. 1875, **$275–$295**; eight-tube candle mold having a graceful lift of the legs, a very unusual form, **$475–$495**.

Chocolate molds: chick pulling cart, **$75–$85**; pig, Riecke & Co., **$75–$85**; teddy bear, **$175–$195**; elephant, **$115–$145**.

Chocolate molds; Father Christmas figures command high prices, especially the Belsnickle versions: 15″ high, Germany, Father Christmas, **$1,200–$1,400**; 13″ high, Germany, **$600–$700**.

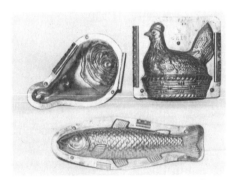

Chocolate molds: ham bone, **$125–$145**; hen on nest, **$85–$95**; fish, **$145–$165**.

Mechanical nutmeg graters: Cast iron, marked "Domestic Nutmeg Grater," **$450–$495**; wood handle, tin grating wheel, paper label, "Common Sense Nutmeg Grater, Patented July 23, 1867," **$450–$495**.

Mechanical nutmeg grater, cast iron, 18th century, and extremely rare type. **$1,200–$1,500**

Mechanical nutmeg graters: tin bellows-shaped grater, **$350–$395**; wood and tin grater, **$275–$295**.

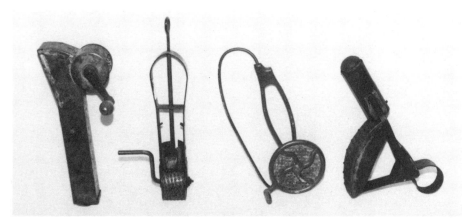

Mechanical nutmeg graters. Tin grater, marked "Davidson Automatic Nutmeg Grater, Pat'd June 2, 1908, Boston, Mass.," **$425–$475**. Tin, spring-action grater, **$325–$350**. Wire handle, iron grater, **$175–$195**. Tin and wood, **$525–$575**.

Nutmeg graters: cardboard box, "Stickney & Poor's, six whole nutmegs," box stored nutmegs, tin grating surface on slide, **$65–$75**. Three-in-one tool – pastry cutter, nutmeg grater, and can opener – tin, iron, and wood, 19th century, **$250–$275**. Tin combination tool, grater, parer, slicer, "Pat. May 2, 1905," **$65–$75**.

Nutmeg graters. *Top*, tin, sliding cover, marked "Wm. Bradley, Pat. Apd. For Lynn," **$250–$275**. *Bottom*, wood, brass crank handle, paper label marked Nutmeg "Mabi," **$175–$195**; tin grater, crank handle, marked "Portable Ginger & Nutmeg Mill, Registered Nov. 11, 1857," **$475–$495**; wood, marked "Nutmeg," **$150–$175**.

Make-dos: there is a collecting category commonly referred to as "make-dos." When a glass or china object was broken, they were often ingeniously restored to usefulness with a tin addition repair. Goblet, **$175–$195**; lamp, **$175–$195**.

Mechanical nutmeg graters. The Little Rhody Grater, wood, **$175–$195**. Tin and wood, barrel-shaped housing on end to slide nutmeg across grating surface, "Pat. 1859," **$165–$185**. The Edgar nutmeg grater, "Pat. Nov. 10, 1896," tin, enamelled wood knobs, **$75–$95**.

4
Stoneware

Many of the stoneware pictures in this chapter are of items in the extensive collection of Al Behr of Carmel, New York, and are used with his kind permission.

Prices of American decorated stoneware began a dramatic rise in the early 1970s and continue to increase. There have been numerous peaks and valleys, but prices continue to rise as supplies of decorated examples decrease.

Stoneware from the potteries of Cowden (Pennsylvania), Stelzenmaier and Burger (New York), and Bennington (Vermont) are especially valuable and are eagerly sought by serious collectors. The most significant factor in recent price increases of major pieces of decorated stoneware has been the emergence of folk art collectors as serious competitors to veteran pottery collectors.

Pennsylvania butter crock, 3-gallon capacity, c. 1865, unsigned, brushed cobalt decoration. **$350–$450**

Decorated Ware

Decorated churns, batter jugs, butter crocks, and pitchers are rare and becoming more expensive each month.

Several years ago, there was a tendency among collectors to seek out the most elaborately decorated pieces that they could find. The pottery marks (often impressed into the piece of stoneware) were a secondary consideration. Many of the hundreds of nineteenth-century stoneware makers were only in business for a brief period. This has created a market for pieces made and signed by these limited-production potteries. A "one or two year mark" on an undecorated piece of stoneware can add considerably to its value.

If a piece of stoneware carries a spectacular decoration, its value normally is not severely altered by restoration. If professionally and correctly restored, an elaborately decorated piece (human figures, lions, deer, scenes) can undergo substantial repairs and still maintain a major portion of its value. A standard floral decoration or simple cobalt bird is negatively affected by restoration, however carefully done.

Mold-Made Pottery

After 1890, most of the utilitarian stoneware produced was molded, rather than hand-thrown. There are still large quantities of molded stoneware jugs and crocks available at reasonable prices. Mold-made pots generally have little decoration; only about 10 percent is signed or marked, although stencils were often used to put a capacity mark and the name of the production pottery on pieces of stoneware.

As the remaining decorated stoneware is sold and enters private collections, the interest in molded stoneware is going to increase and prices will rise. It might be a good investment to put away a few exceptional molded pieces in perfect condition as a hedge against the future market.

Miniature jug, half-pint, unsigned, unusual decoration. **$140–$165**

Lard crock, half-gallon, c. 1875, J. Hamilton and Co., Greensboro, Pennsylvania. **$175–$200**

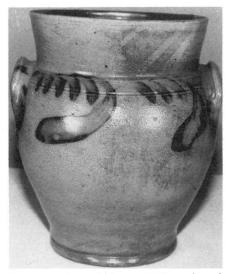

Pennsylvania ovoid jar, c. 1850, unsigned, brush decoration. **$450–$500**

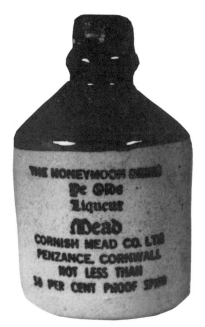

THE HONEYMOON DRINK
Ye Olde
Liqueur
Mead
CORNISH MEAD CO. LTD
PENZANCE, CORNWALL
NOT LESS THAN
30 PER CENT PROOF SPIRIT

OI BE ALL THE WAY FROM CHEDDAR

Miniature jug, possibly English in origin. **$25–$30**

Three-gallon Pennsylvania butter crock with lid, unsigned, c. 1865. **$400–$500**

Pennsylvania butter crock, c. 1865, 1½-gallon size, brush decoration. **$400–$500**

Pennsylvania butter crock cover or lid, tulip decoration. **$175–$200**

Miniature pitcher, 3″ tall, c. 1900, unsigned. **$50–$55**

Miniature molasses jug, molded, unsigned. **$20–$25**

Butter crock, two-gallon, c. 1865, unsigned, brushed decoration. **$300–$335**

Match holder/striker, 2½″ tall, c. 1885, unsigned. **$75–$85**

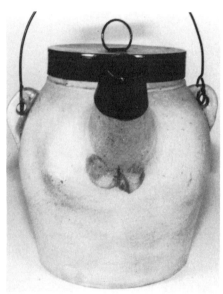

Pennsylvania batter pail, one-gallon, Cowden and Wilcox, Harrisburg, Pennsylvania, brush decoration. **$1600–$1800**

One-gallon batter pail, original lids, marked "F. H. Cowden," stencilled decoration on back, c. 1879. **$600–$650**

Contemporary stoneware made by R. H. Diebball of Washington, Michigan. **$40–$80** each

Half-pint jug, 7″ tall, mid-nineteenth century. **$85–$100**

Stoneware bottle, 10″ tall, weighs 3 pounds, molded. **$20–$25**

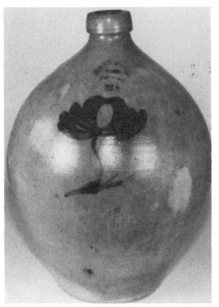

Two-gallon ovoid jug, c. 1829, Clark and Fox, Athens, New York. **$325–$350**

Mug, c. 1870, pewter lid, hand thrown, unsigned. **$100–$115**

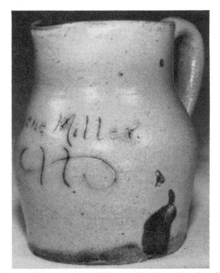

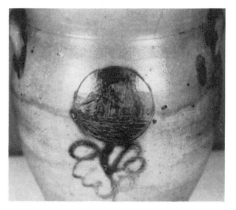

Unsigned two-gallon jar, 12″ tall, c. 1809, incised drawing of a battleship. **$3000–$3500**

One-pint presentation pitcher, incised name of "Eugene Miller," approximately 5″ tall, c. 1860–1870. **$575–$600**

Reverse side of jar, showing simple brushed decoration.

Stoneware mugs, made at Whites Utica (New York) Pottery, c. 1885, unsigned. **$85–$100** each

Two-gallon ovoid jug, c. 1813, N. Clark, Athens, New York, rare and early mark. **$325–$450**

Four-gallon crock, c. 1868, New York Stoneware Co., Ft. Edward, New York. **$425–$575**

Three-gallon crock, c. 1870, unsigned, "chicken pecking corn" decoration. **$475–$575**

Four-gallon jug, c. 1867–1872, Haxstun Ottman and Co., Ft. Edward, New York. **$525–$600**

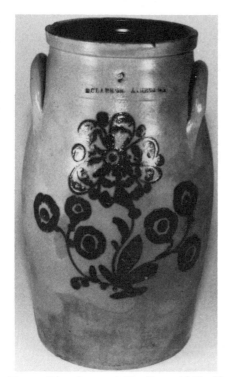

Two-gallon crock, 9″ tall, c. 1882–1886, N. A. White & Son, Utica, New York. **$575–$775**

Two-gallon churn, 14″ tall, c. 1866, N. Clark Jr., Athens, New York. **$1500–$1800**

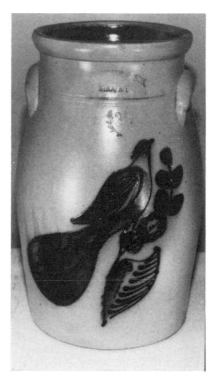

Two-gallon crock, c. 1875, unsigned, probably New Jersey in origin. **$325–$450**

Three-gallon churn, 15″ tall, c. 1882, A. White & Son, Utica, New York. **$1400–$1800**

Half-gallon preserve jar, unsigned, c. 1865–1880, probably from West Virginia or Pennsylvania. **$2500–$3000**

Four-gallon jar with sailing ship, probably from Morgantown, West Virginia, c. 1850. **$6500–$7500**

Two contemporary stoneware jars from Beaumont Pottery, York, Maine, **$35–$45** each

Utica, New York, stoneware mugs, dated 1894. **$150–$250** each

Rear of jar, showing flag growing out of a tulip vine.

One-pint jug, 7″ tall, c. 1807–1815, Paul Cushmans, Albany, New York. **$600–$675**

One-gallon jug, c. 1859–1861, Ft. Edward, New York. **$375–$425**

Ovoid jug, one-gallon, c. 1809, Commeraws/Stoneware, New York, incised and impressed decoration. **$2800–$3200**

Six-gallon crock, c. 1849–1856, Whites, Binghamton, New York. **$750–$825**

Two-gallon Bennington, Vermont, jar, ovoid, c. 1823. **$700–$800**

Pennsylvania cooler, 6–8 gallon, c. 1860, unsigned. **$875–$1000**

Three-gallon churn, c. 1865–1867, J. A. and C. W. Underwood, Ft. Edward, New York, stump and peacock decoration. **$2000–$2500**

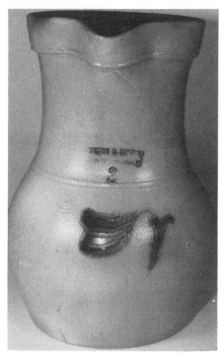

Two-gallon pitcher, Norton and Fenton, E. Bennington, Vermont, c. 1844–1847, rare form. **$3500–$4000**

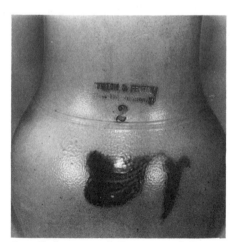

Detail, impressed Norton and Fenton pitcher.

Unusual molded pitcher, c. 1885–1895, possibly Whites Pottery, Utica, New York. **$225–$275**

Miniature mug, c. 1890, unsigned, possibly Midwestern, lighthouse design. **$75–$90**

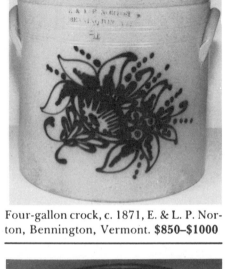

Four-gallon crock, c. 1871, E. & L. P. Norton, Bennington, Vermont. **$850–$1000**

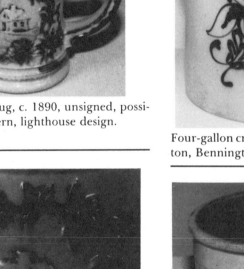

Detail, lighthouse mug.

Unsigned one-gallon jar. **$175–$225**

New York state bird crock. **$300–$350**

Greensboro, Pennsylvania, preserve jar.
$150–$175

Two-gallon vendor's jug. **$175–$200**

One-gallon J. & E. Norton bird pitcher.
$1900–$2500

Rare Cowden and Wilcox two-gallon
pheasant jug. **$6000–$6500**

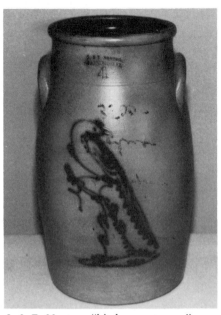

J. & E. Norton, "bird on a stump."
$2000–$2500

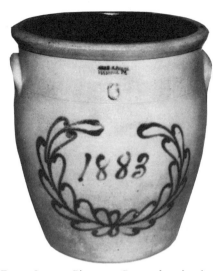

Evan Jones, Pittston, Pennsylvania, jar, dated 1883. **$750–$950**

One-gallon gooney bird jar, marked "Cortland." **$1900–$2100**

One-gallon crock, Whites Utica, canal boat. **$2000–$2400**

Pennsylvania preserve jar, brush decoration. **$135–$165** each

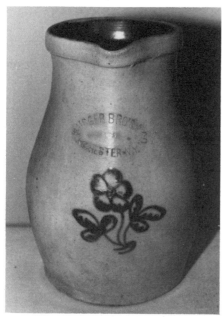

One-gallon pitcher marked "Burger Bros. & Co., Rochester, N.Y." **$1100–$1300**

Rare six-gallon cooler marked Bennington Factory, c. 1823. **$3000–$4000**

Crock with frolicking horse, 3-gallon capacity, New York City mark. **$3900–$4500**

One-gallon batter pail, flower on front, marked "Cowden and Wilcox" on back. **$2200–$2400**

New Geneva, Pennsylvania, jar. **$225–$275**

Cowden and Wilcox batter pail, brushed grapes decoration. **$3200–$3700**

One-gallon Pennsylvania unsigned pitcher, c. 1865. **$425–$475**

One-gallon jar marked "Porter Pleasantville," c. 1870. **$500–$550**

One-gallon pitcher, Whites Utica, New York, c. 1865. **$375–$425**

Half-gallon unsigned Pennsylvania pitcher. **$475–$525**

Early two-gallon ovoid jug, marked "C. Crolius Manufacturer, N.Y." **$900–$1300**

Large stein, inn scene, attributed to Whites Utica. **$250–$275**

Five-gallon crock, leaping deer decoration, C. W. Braun, Buffalo, New York. **$3000–$3500**

Basket of flowers, W. A. Lewis, Gatesville, New York. **$1700–$2000**

One-gallon pitcher, W. A. Standish, Taunton, Massachusetts, rare piece. **$1800–$2000**

Two-gallon eagle jar, William Warner, W. Troy, New York. **$3500–$4000**

Stoneware bottles, molded. **$90–$110** each

Incised bird and flower, L. Norton & Son, Bennington, Vermont. **$5500–$6000**

Molded cake crock with hunting scene, probably Whites Utica. **$175–$225**

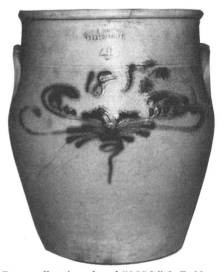

Four-gallon jar, dated "1856," J. E. Norton. **$750–$850**

Molded stoneware dog doorstop, Ebey Pottery, Winchester, Illinois. **$125–$150**

Molded stoneware pipes, nineteenth century, New England. **$30–$50** each

Excellent cross-section of American stoneware from the nineteenth century. Pieces range from an 1830s ovoid jug to a molded stoneware jar with a "drop" handle made c. 1900.

Stoneware birdhouse, White Hall, Illinois. **$125–$150**

Molded stoneware mug with applied handle. **$60–$65**

Molded stoneware cake crock with lid, White Hall, Illinois. **$250–$300**

Molded stoneware mixing bowls. **$15–$35** each

Charm jar; molded stoneware jar covered with another coat of clay and then a variety of everyday items. **$50–$75**

Stoneware chicken waterer, Red Wing, Minnesota. **$40-$50**

Water cooler, Monmouth, Illinois. **$65–$85** each

Collection of contemporary stoneware. **$12–$15** each

Sponge-decorated molded stoneware bowl. **$20–$28**

Molded mixing bowl. **$18–$24**

Sponge-decorated molded stoneware. **$90–$150** each

Molded stoneware canning jar. **$16–$20**

Cross-section of molded stoneware made in the late nineteenth and early twentieth centuries.

Molded stoneware bowls. **$15–$20** each

Stoneware rolling pin with maple handles, unmarked. **$55–$70**

Molded pitcher, late nineteenth century. **$100–$150**

Mugs and stoneware pitcher, molded, seven-piece set. **$65–$80**

5
Decoys

This chapter was prepared by John and Mary Purvis, nationally known dealers in waterfowl decoys. They participate in many shows and have an extensive mail-order business at 50609 Bell Fort Court, New Baltimore, MI 48047; 313-725-2179.
Decoy prices followed by an asterisk (*) indicate actual auction selling prices.

Decoy collecting is neither new nor a passing fancy. The folksy wooden sculptures have long attracted both man and bird. In recent times, their popularity has been growing dramatically. In 1987, one decoy sold at auction for more than $300,000. At the same time, fine examples of decoy art are available from $25 to a few hundred dollars.

Prices definitely are rising. Scarcity is a threat. "Finds" are fewer, almost non-existent in some locales. As the credentials of the decoy collector improve, quality overshadows quantity as a standard. "Unknown" carvers are continually "discovered,"

Black duck, Benjamin Holmes carver, Stratford, Connecticut; hollow decoy with scratch paint, excellent condition. **$20,000***

investigated, traced, and collected. Collectors are multiplying.

The "working" decoy is folk art with a twist: an item made for effectiveness, to be used, beauty was not required. As waterfowl was often a dietary staple, the decoy had to work! Proof of the decoy and a compliment to the carver was success on the hunt. This was true whether the decoy was a mound of mud with a stick for a head or a carefully crafted formation of wood. Practicality dictated material, color and shape. Variety was limited only by the imagination and ability of the carver.

A Brief History

Decoys were used prior to the birth of Christ. The oldest known North American decoy exceeds one thousand years in age. At the turn of the century, there were seemingly as many carvers as hunters. Almost every old hunter carved a few or a "rig" for himself or his friends. Many of them have become the "unknown" carvers we investigate today. The majority of collectible decoys were made by a smaller number of carvers who "did business," producing many rigs for themselves, friends, or to sell. Large factories were also mass producing decoys of varying quality during this period.

U.S. and Canadian decoys are commonly categorized by region (Nova Scotia, Louisiana, North Carolina, etc.) or by carver. Regional types developed for specific reasons: rough or smooth water; ocean, lake or marsh. The maker might emphasize height, weight, size, color, wing, or tail. Available wood supplies often dictated size or method of construction. Style often varied during the life of the carver as his ideas and needs changed. His cus-

tomers' desires also shaped the type of decoy he made. Often, a decoy made in one area was carried to another to add confusion to identification.

Factory-made decoys were used and are found in all regions. Mass-carved on duplicating lathes although often hand-painted, these decoys were inexpensive and readily available. The total number of factories in operation is unknown, but certainly numbers several hundred in and out of business over the years. These factories produced hundreds of thousands of decoys. Quality varied from horrid to extra fine and, occasionally, a factory introduced a unique (collectible) feature like flap wings or a mechanical caller. With the exception of Mason decoys, few factory-made birds command the prices that hand-carved decoys do.

The joint U.S./Canadian introduction of bag limits in 1918 effectively ended "market" hunting, which flourished after the expansion of the railroads in the late nineteenth century. Many decoys made prior to that time apparently were destroyed or abandoned when no longer needed. Hunting changed from business to sport. Individual carvers and factories continued to produce, but in far smaller quantities.

Carvers began devoting more time to enhancing decoy details to more perfectly imitate the quarry. This trend continues today.

Tips for Collectors

This brief history hints at warnings for beginning collectors.

1. No one knows all about all decoys from all areas, despite what they might say.
2. No one even knows all about all

decoys from one area.
3. Potentially, a beginner could be at the mercy of the expert.

Common factors affecting decoy price: hand carved or factory; paint condition; physical condition; carver name and current popularity; age; uniqueness; written reference; sellers *opinion* of value; cost to seller. Realistically, there are *no* set prices. Buyer beware? Certainly. Is it safe to collect – or even buy one decoy? By all means, *yes* – if a buyer follows one simple beginner's rule:

Buy only what you like and can afford.

Simple, safe, there are no bad buys. A *reasonable* investment like this in an expansive and intensive market can most always be recouped. If trustworthy advice is available, avail! As a collection grows, there is time to read books, go to auctions, meet other collectors, specialize. Naturally, when buying decoys strictly for investment, one should follow sound investment principles. Be warned, however, that some mushy sentiment will probably sneak in – and why not? Decoys are fun, pretty, keepable, and visible.

Materials and Conditon

Materials. Mostly wood – all flavors tried; cork; canvas over wire; stuffed canvas; metal, printed paper; papier mâché; palm fronds; reeds; plastic; Styrofoam. Values normally descend in that order.

Paint. Good original paint is a value plus. But, working decoys were *used*, often needed and got new paint. Some hunters repainted annually. Working paint can add a "mystique" factor.

Age. We believe the importance of decoy age should be one of personal

collection preference. Some fine old-time carvers were active in the 1960s; a few still are.

Condition. Working decoys are rarely found in perfect condition. Some "mantle" birds or never-used birds do show up. Few of us will own these. Accept some wear as character of the decoy. Shot holes are not uncommon, necks and bills broke and were repaired. Eyes fell out. Not fatal.

Specialized Decoys

New Carvings. Beautiful decoys are being carved today – with much detail, beautiful paint, often high prices. These are "decoratives," not to be confused with "working decoys." The latter is not afraid of water. The new decoratives are expensive and, to date, an active resale market is not established.

Taiwan Specials. Bright, smooth, with gaudy paint. Gift and department stores. Mass produced. *Zero* collector value.

Reed Decoys. If you find one, it must be new. If not in a collection, museum, or the like, and is available to you, hire a detective to check the provenance.

Forgeries. They exist. Mexico, Bolivia, Holland make and export "aged" decoys. Experience shows that they tend to "just look wrong." Colors are off. Wear simulated. They may seem genuine, but value very slight.

Fish Decoys. Fairly recent area of collection. We suggest reading *The Fish Decoy* (vols. I, II) by the Kimballs, and beginners should only buy for pleasure. Prices of ice fishing decoys have climbed very fast. There *are* forgeries of the big names. We have an assortment we call "affordable/collectible/enjoyable." No big names, just fun.

No big expense. Stick to these unless you plan a quick, hard study.

Shorebirds. Limited availability of genuine old shorebirds. They are expensive. Lots of very attractive, affordable shorebirds being made today. Not great growth items, but they look good.

Pintail drake, Bert Graves carver, Peoria, Illinois; thin strip of lead on the bottom to weight the duck upright in water. **$1500***

Pintail drake, Joe Lincoln carver, Accord, Massachusetts. **$13,000***.

Eider drake, Jesse Clayton Obed carver, Cape Negro, Nova Scotia. **$3000***

Shorebird, black-breasted plover, George Boyd, Seabrook, New Hampshire. **$2500***

Bluebill drake, Elmer Crowell carver, East Harwich, Massachusetts, **$6000***. One Crowell decoy sold for over **$300,000**.

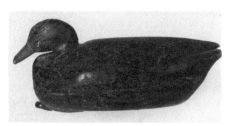

Black duck, Nathan Cobb, Cobbs Island, Virginia; original worn paint, with the typical grooved carving to the tail. **$7500***

Bluebill drake, James Holly carver, Susquehana Flats, Maryland. **$1000***

Shorebirds. Yellowlegs, William Bowman, Lawrence, Long Island; sandpiper, Elmer Crowell carver. **$7000–$8000*** each

Right, canvasback drake, Nick Purdo and Pecor Fox carvers, Mt. Clemens, Michigan; balsa body, hardwood head; "working" repaint, **$65–$100**. *Left*, canvasback drake, William Finkel carver, Algonac, Michigan, "repaint," **$75–$150**.

Rear, redhead drake, Tom Chambers carver, Toronto, Ontario; "short body" model. Chambers is the best known Canadian carver up to **$2000***;more for other models. *Foreground*, black duck, John R. Wells (JRW) carver, Toronto, Ontario, **$700**. Some Wells decoys recently sold for over **$5000** at auction.

Left, redhead drake, maker unknown, layered body, **$55–$80**. *Right*, redhead drake, Ralph Reghi carver, Detroit, Michigan; paint is original, good condition, well-known Michigan carver. Reghi signed this decoy for the owner and indicated that it was made about 1929, **$400–$600**.

Merganser, Willie Ross carver, Chebeaque Island, Maine. **$3500***

Rear, canvasback drake, Ben Schmidt carver, Centerline, Michigan; **$450–$700**. *Foreground*, mallard hen, Tom Schroeder carver, Michigan; rare form, super paint, **$2000–$3000**.

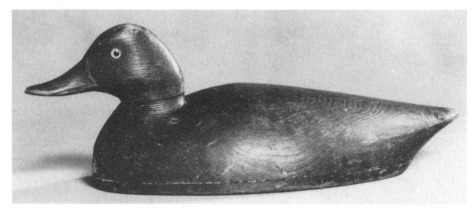

Bluebill, Robert Renardson carver, Toronto, Ontario; c. 1850, hollow, fine condition. Renardson is an early carver, recently "rediscovered," and his decoys are increasing rapidly in value. **$500–$1000**

Bluebills, George "Red" Weir carver, Hamilton, Ontario; hollow, multi-piece bodies. **$90–$150** each

Rear, mallard hen, Victor Animal Trap Co., Pascagoula, Mississippi; original paint, near mint condition, **$45–$60**. *Foreground*, mallard drake, probably Pratt Mgf. Co., Joliet, Illinois. The lines around the decoy bodies are marks from the lathe. "Factory" decoy values diminish dramatically as the quality of condition and paint goes down. **$45–$60**

Canvasback, Fred Dolsen, Martins Islands, Lake St. Clair, rare, original paint. **$700+**

Bluebills, George Warin carver, Toronto, Ontario, late 19th century; Warin known for mallards, blacks, canvasbacks and great paint jobs. **$300–$3000+**

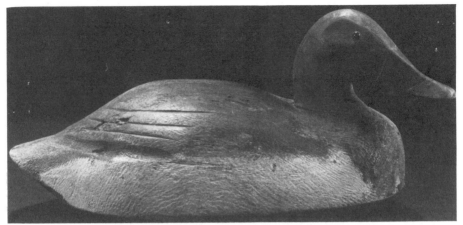

Canvasback, carver unknown, probably Michigan in origin. **$100–$200**

Underside. Many decoys were hollowed out to reduce weight. Some were left open, others closed with a bottom board.

Rear, redhead drake, Mason Decoy Factory, Detroit, Michigan, 1894–1924; challenge grade, worn but clear original paint, **$300–$500**. *Foreground*, Mason standard grade (paint eye model), original paint with slight wear, **$150–$250**.

Rear, Mason canvasback drake, Seneca Lake model, significant repaint, **$200–$300**. *Foreground*, Mason Premier Grade; worn original paint, slight body damage, **$300–$500** (much more in fine condition).

Canvasback drake, Reg Marksby carver, Blenheim, Ontario; original paint, excellent condition. Worth up to **$800** in this condition; Marksby decoys in lesser condition, **$50–$150** range.

Left, Greenwing teal, Ernest Vidacovich carver, Avondale, Louisiana, **$700***. *Right*, pintail drake, Mike Frady carver, New Orleans, Louisiana, **$250***.

Canvasback drake, Gus Modde carver, Wallaceburg, Ontario; good example of large, strong, working decoys used on Lake St. Clair for deep water shooting, not rare. **$50–$100**

Rail or Gallinulle, maker unknown, Canadian in origin, classic form, piece of folk art. **$5000**

Bluebill drake, Russ Smith carver, Blenheim, Ontario. **$100–$150**

Rear, canvasback drake, maker unknown, Lake St. Clair, **$75–$125**. *Foreground*, bluebill drake, "Doc" Baumgartner carver, Houghton Lake, Michigan, **$75–$125**.

Rear, canvasback drake, Harold Jennett, Mt. Clemens, Michigan; value is in "folksiness" and scarcity, **$50–$75**. *Foreground*, black duck, Art Brown, Toronto; mellow old paint, **$400–$600**.

Rear, Merganser, maker unknown found at Ontario Flea Market, possibly from Nova Scotia, partial cork body, **$300–$500**. *Foreground*, Merganser, Nova Scotia, maker unknown, old paint, staples holding neck, bill repair, leather crest. **$300–$500**

Rear, bluebill drake, attributed to Chris Smith, founder of Chris Craft Boats, Algonac, Michigan; late 1800s, much overpaint, general wear, still a sound decoy, **$300–$500**. *Foreground*, golden-eye drake, "Budgie" Sampier, Pearl Beach, Michigan; excellent old bobtail, hollow, many repaints, c. 1890, **$200–$350**.

Canvasback drakes, unknown carvers, probably from Lake Erie area; not of significant value, but both are collectible. **$50–$75** each

Black duck and drake pintail, Charles Perdew carver, Henry, Illinois; Illinois River style, excellent condition. **$3500–$4500*** each

Rear, confidence decoy, Grebe or Coot, unknown carver, found in Canada, **$600–$800**. *Foreground*, bluebill drake, attributed to Lou Birch, Chincoteaque, Virginia; old working repaint, worn, painted eye, **$200–$300**.

Merganser, maker unknown, found in Kent County, Ontario; heavily used. **$200–$300**

Canada goose, Dupe-A-Goose decoys, Seattle, Washington; these are cardboard "silhouettes" that spread apart for use, fold flat for carrying. The picture is printed on the cardboard with a fold out stake for standing up. **$20–$40**

Rear, black duck, George Harris, Gores Landing, Ontario; great scratch paint, original condition, unusual long, slim body with high head, **$300–$400**. *Foreground*, redhead hen, maker unknown, Lake St. Clair, fine wood-tone finish, no eyes, **$100–$200**.

Canada Goose, attributed to Harry Shourds, Tuckerton, N.J.; c. 1910; hollow, old repaint. **$300–$500+**

Left, bluebill drake, attributed to David Ward, Toronto, Ontario; late 1800s, **$700–$1000**. *Right*, bluebill, Dan Bartlett, Prince Edward County, Ontario; paint around tack for eye, **$600–$800**.

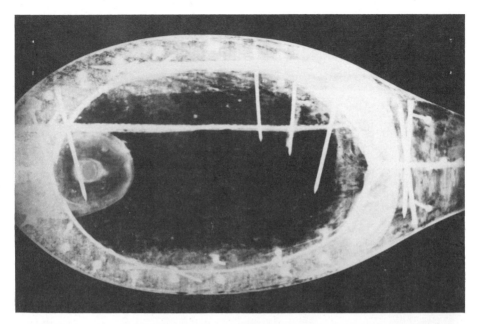

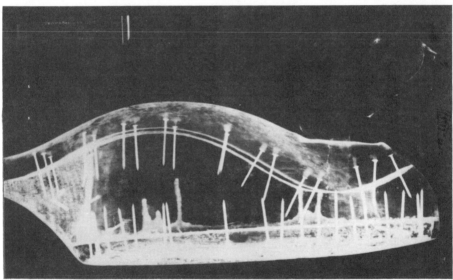

Prints from x-rays of a decoy, Dodge Decoy Factory, Detroit, c. 1895. Originally, the decoy had a three-piece body held together by a few nails and glue. Hard use separated the pieces and additional nails were added over the years. *Top*, nails from the side repair a split. Only a very few nails were visible without the x-rays.

Large canvasback, **$400–$600**; small buf-flehead, **$100–$200**. Both unique.

Canvasback drake, maker unknown, Lake St. Clair, c. 1875; found in Ontario, but probably U.S. in origin. **$500+**

Far left rear, dove decoy, printed cardboard, "DunCoy" on side, **$40–$60**. *Left rear*, miniature goose, Ira Hudson carver, mint condition, **$100–$300**. *Left center*, "salesman's sample size" papier mâché mallard, **$25–$45** (in recent years, these have been reproduced). *Right*, English pigeon decoy, **$200–$300**.

Rear, redhead drake, maker unknown, found in Southwest Ontario; "working" repaint, good condition, **$40–$60**. *Foreground*, bluebill drake, H. H. Ackerman carver, Trenton, Michigan, prolific carver. **$45–$75**

Pair of ringnecks (bluebills), Jim Barr carver, Hamilton, Ontario; Most decoys from this area are found with a great deal of overpaint. **$90–$250**

6
Amish Dolls

This section was prepared by Linda Grunewald and shows numerous examples from her collection and inventory. She has sold Amish dolls by mail order to collectors, dealers, and museums all over the world for the past five years. To receive a current list with color photos of early Amish dolls and toys, send $4 (refundable with first order) to Linda Grunewald, Amish Doll Color List, P.O. Box 311-a, Utica, Michigan 48087.

Amish dolls and other playthings demonstrate the real meaning of folk art: no two are exactly alike. They were made for personal use from a myriad of leftover bits of everyday life.

Some background of the Amish themselves is necessary in order to understand their doll- and toy-making. Since the sixteenth century, the Amish have lived plain lives, without the world's modern machines and conveniences, because of their strict religious beliefs. Many people are surprised to find that antique Amish dolls are not stitched by

Amish doll, 10"; c. 1920, Missouri. Cotton batting stuffed. **$195–$250**

hand. Amish women have been using the treadle machine for most all sewing projects since its invention in the late 1800s.

Featureless Faces

Why Amish dolls usually have no facial features is probably lost in history. There is nothing in writing that forbids it, but it is generally felt that putting a face on a doll would be making a graven image, which is a sin. However, many Amish dolls are found with embroidered or crudely painted-on faces, usually done by a child's hand.

Construction and Dating

Body styles vary greatly. Swartzenruber dolls from Ohio usually have no arms and legs, and are made of dark fabrics. Without clothing, they resemble potatoes. Sometimes arms have been sewn into the dress sleeves and sometimes empty sleeves dangle from the body. Most Amish dolls have arms and legs sewn onto the trunk. Other body styles are flat, almost like a pancake. Some are rounded out like a real baby and have buttons sewn onto the arms and legs that give them jointed movement. Dolls of this type seem to be made from a pattern and were most plentiful after 1930.

The stuffing inside a doll is a clue to its age. Rags, cotton batting, and unwashed field or seed cotton were most commonly used. The only way to determine what stuffing was used is to dissect it a little. In an unobtrusive spot, such as under the clothing at the side of the trunk, carefully open the side seam a few stitches with a dull razor blade. Make sure not to cut the material. With a needle inserted inside the opening, pull out a tiny bit of stuffing and examine it. Push the stuffing back inside the doll and stitch up the opening with small stitches of matching thread. Sawdust and seed cotton were used before cotton batting. Homespun wool rag strips are older than factory-made materials. Solid polyester filling would tell you that the doll is not very old.

These dolls were meant to be played with and, along the way, may have lost some stuffing. Newer stuffing may have been inserted at a later date. As long as the doll still retains at least 75 percent of its original stuffing, I would not consider this a major detriment in determining worth. If more than 25 percent new stuffing has been added, the doll's value might be lower.

While you have the doll open, look along the stitching line at the material along the inside selvage. If it is old, it should be lighter in color than the outside body fabric. Since most Amish dolls were made of white cotton, you should see a whiter color inside the entire length of the doll's stitching line wherever you may open it, because it has not been exposed to dirt. This would be hard to fake. New dolls made of old cloth would be the same color inside the stitching line as out. The only trouble in using this method to determine the age of the doll is that you cannot dissect it before you buy it. If you buy from reputable dealers, they will stand behind their merchandise.

New reproduction dolls being made by the Amish and others today for resale should not pose a problem: cloth ages much like wood and should be worn in areas where hands have touched it over the years, but not worn evenly over the entire doll as if the fabric had been chemically aged.

Darker spots should occur on exposed areas; holes may appear in worn spots.

Workmanship

The actual quality of sewing and workmanship in the dolls varies. Most are fairly crude, often done quickly as a first venture into sewing by a young girl. Amish dolls were not given the same painstaking attention that Amish quilts received.

Doll clothing is usually made of solid, dark, or bright colors; the Mennonites used tiny prints. Check to see if the clothes are old. Most dolls have been redressed over the years. Hats, bonnets and booties are sometimes later additions on old dolls.

Stuffed Animals

Amish stuffed animals are a breed of their own. Most are cats, dogs, horses, and rabbits—animals that would be common on a farm. They are fat little four-legged creatures that sometimes have button eyes or sewn-on faces. The same methods used in determining the age of a doll can be used on the stuffed animals.

Collecting Guidelines

The largest Amish settlements are in Pennsylvania, Ohio, and Indiana. Smaller groups can be found in Michigan, Iowa, and Missouri. You might have luck finding an old doll or toy in these areas, but usually you will find only the new ones. Antique shops, shows and auctions are your best sources.

Determining a doll's value encompasses many things. Generally speaking, church dolls, which are approximately 7 inches tall and were taken to long church services to amuse the baby, and twins are the rarest. Broth-er and sister dolls and boys are harder to find than single girl dolls. Next, you must take into account the doll's age. Usually the older the doll, the more it's worth. Size may also be a factor. Typically, the bigger the doll, the greater its value unless it is a church doll. Then, smaller is more desirable.

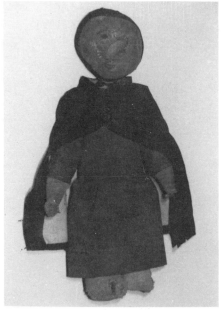

Amish doll, 13½"; c. 1890, Indiana. Stuffed with homespun wool rag strips. Worn head still has traces of a painted-on face. **$275–$350**

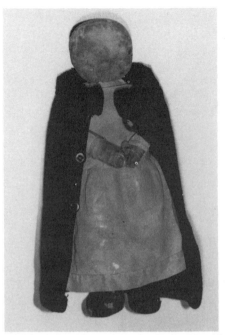

Amish doll, 16"; c. 1890. Stuffed with old cotton rags; early wool stockings sewn on; wool cape. **$275–$350**

Amish church doll, 7"; c. 1900, Ohio. Cotton gauze body with cotton rag stuffing. **$275–$350**

Amish church doll, 7½"; c. 1890, Indiana. Seed-cotton stuffing. **$275–$350**

Amish boy church doll, 9¼"; c. 1920, Missouri. Seed-cotton stuffed; newer clothes. **$195–$250**

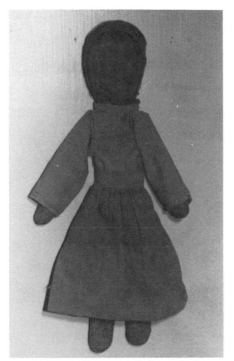

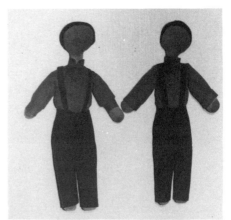

Amish twin boys, 12½"; c. 1920, Pennsylvania. Cheesecloth bodies; seed-cotton stuffed; caps are a later addition. **$500–$575**, pair

Amish doll, 14"; c. 1920, Missouri. Cotton rag stuffed, **$195–$250**

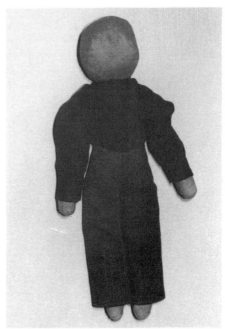

Amish brother doll, 17"; c. 1920, Missouri. Cotton rag stuffing; newer clothes. **$200–$275**

Amish doll, 17"; c. 1920, Missouri. Cotton rag stuffing; cotton stockings sewn on; newer dress. **$200–$275**

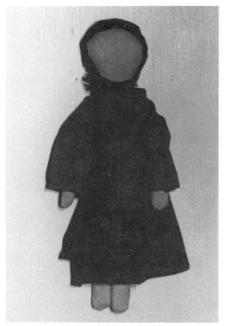

Amish doll, 12½"; c. 1920, Missouri. Wool rag stuffing. **$195–$250**

Amish boy doll, 12"; c. 1920, Missouri. Seed cotton stuffing. **$195–$250**

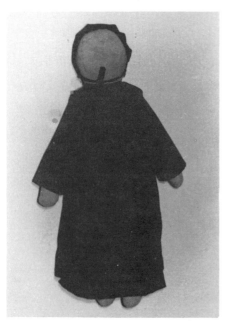

Amish doll, 17"; c. 1920, Missouri. Cotton rag stuffing. **$200–$275**

Amish boy doll, 12½"; c. 1920, Missouri. Seed cotton stuffing. **$195–$250**

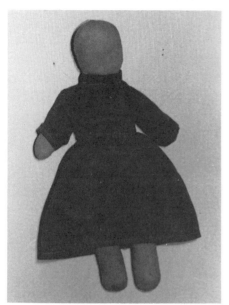

Amish doll, 11"; c. 1920, Missouri. Feed sack body; cotton string rag stuffing; a stick of wood is inside for support. **$155–$195**

Amish girl doll, 12"; c. 1920, Missouri. Feed sack body; cotton string rag stuffing; stockings and wool shoes added at a later date. **$155–$195**

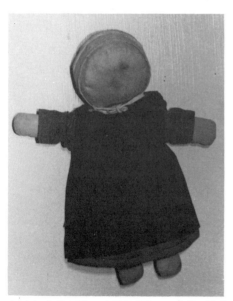

Amish doll, 12"; c. 1930, Missouri. Stuffed with rags sewn into a cord for rug braiding. **$155–$195**

Amish doll, 11"; c. 1930, Missouri. Cotton rag stuffing. **$135–$175**

Amish doll, 15"; c. 1930, Missouri. Floppy rag ball head; cotton rag stuffing. **$155–$195**

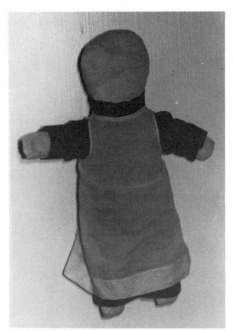

Amish doll, 13"; c. 1930, Missouri. Cotton rag stuffing. **$155–$195**

Amish doll, 12½"; c. 1930, Missouri. Lumpy cotton batting stuffing. **$135–$175**

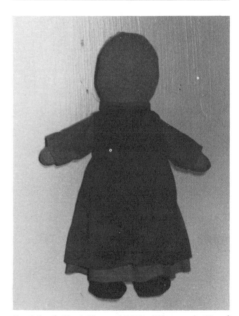

Amish doll, 12"; c. 1920, Missouri. Feed sack body, cotton string rag stuffing. Stockings and wool shoes are later additions. **$155–$195**

Amish doll, 14″; c. 1920, Missouri. Cotton rag stuffing. **$155 – $195**

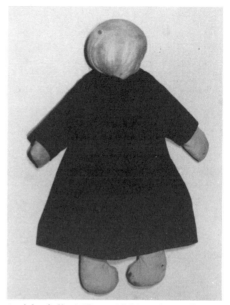

Amish doll, 16″; c. 1930, Missouri. Rag ball head is self-supported; cotton rag stuffing. **$135–$175**

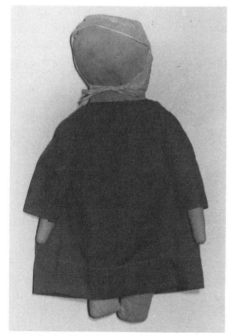

Amish doll, 19″; c. 1930, Michigan. Stuffed with strips of an old cotton blanket. **$135–$175**

Amish boy doll's woolen, drop-front britches; c. 1920. **$25–$35**

121

Amish cotton stuffed dog; c. 1920.
$90–$100

Amish stuffed animals: jointed bear and a dog. Cotton bodies with cotton rag stuffing. **$90–$100** each

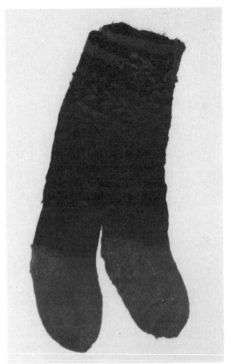

Amish child's wool, hand-knit stockings with decorative tops; c. 1900. Decorative top stockings came almost solely from Pennsylvania. **$90–$100**, pair

Mennonite straw-stuffed dog; wool covering; c. 1920. **$90–$100**

7
Country Baskets

F ew collectors paid much attention to baskets prior to the 1970s. They were plentiful and relatively inexpensive. Then, home decorating magazines began to show readers how baskets could be used with collections of country antiques. Prices increased rapidly and the supply of "old" baskets in good repair diminished.

Woven Splint Baskets

Almost all baskets were made by hand before 1890. With the exception of Nantucket baskets, most American baskets were made of ash or white oak splint. The splint was cut, soaked, and

Tightly woven buttocks basket, oak splint stained a deep brown, shows wear. **$160–$185**

woven into utilitarian baskets that were sold one at a time by traveling salespeople or in rural and urban general stores.

Machines that cut splint into thick, wide strips came into use in the early 1890s. Each splint cut by machine is identical to every other piece in a basket. Factories replaced local basket makers very quickly; few basket weavers continued to ply their trade into the twentieth century.

Country baskets were designed to be used on a regular basis. If the bottom of a basket fell out or a handle snapped, it was rarely repaired. By today's standards, a basket that is fifty to sixty years old can be classified as an antique. Baskets are difficult to date because styles and construction techniques of hand-crafted examples changed little over the years.

Nantucket Lightship Baskets

Nantucket baskets are made from rattan, imported from the Philippines, and have turned wooden bottoms and movable or "drop" handles. Nantucket baskets were made in a variety of sizes and several *nests* — groups of baskets in graduated sizes — have survived.

Very few baskets were ever signed by their makers. But many of the Nantucket Lightship baskets made between 1900 and the early 1930s were "signed"; paper labels with the makers name were glued to the bottoms of baskets. Few of these baskets survive with the paper labels intact.

Shaker Baskets

The Shakers wove many baskets around wooden molds. Their baskets are well made and never crudely constructed. The Shakers began selling their baskets outside their communities in the early 1800s and continued to offer them until about 1880. Few of the ash or oak baskets were ever signed.

Today, many baskets that were tightly woven over a mold are advertised as "Shaker." It is extremely difficult to be certain.

Wicker and Willow Baskets

Many wicker baskets were factory made and imported in huge quantities from the 1890s until the present. When the bark is removed (peeled) from the willow branches and made into a basket it is called a willow basket. Willow is wicker without the bark.

Contemporary vs. Antique Baskets

With the growing interest in handcrafted ash and oak baskets, there has been an increase in the number of skilled craftspeople weaving country baskets. Several of these makers are producing investment-quality baskets that will create major league problems for the next generation of collectors when the baskets begin to turn up at auctions and in shops.

Meanwhile, a collector is not likely to find a Shaker seed box or a painted pine cupboard at a roadside antiques shop in Nebraska or Idaho. But it *is* always possible to find an unusual basket form almost anywhere. Baskets are discovered at tag sales in Grosse Point, Michigan, and farm closeout sales in Hereford, North Carolina.

The value of a country basket is enhanced dramatically if it carries a painted finish. Painted baskets are uncommon and should be evaluated much like a piece of painted furniture. They should show wear and general signs of use. A utilitarian basket with pristine paint should immediately be suspect.

As we mentioned before, it is extremely difficult to accurately date a basket form if it is constructed with the same techniques used by nineteenth-century basket makers. A basket that was heavily used for 5 years could appear to be 75 years old, with little opportunity for debate.

Ash splint basket with a "kicked in" or demijohn bottom, swing or drop handle. **$300–$375**

Rye basket, used raise dough; Pennsylvania. **$110–$125**

Half-basket, hickory handle, oak splint, wrapped handle. **$200–$250**

Market basket, open-weave bottom, oak splint. **$95–$110**

Close-up of "drop" handle.

A "kicked in" bottom allowed the load in the basket to be evenly distributed around the sides, rather than falling through the center.

Shaker sewing basket with four attached compartments for sewing utensils, New England; sold in the Sisters' shops at several communities. **$500–$585**

Finely woven feather-type basket with a slide lid, New England. **$350–$400**

Market basket with two drop handles, early twentieth century. **$100–$130**

Willow gathering basket, twentieth century. **$45–$60**

Drop-handled market basket, Native American, twentieth century. **$50–$60**

Drop-handled basket, probably made in Wisconsin or Michigan, c. 1930–1940. $45–$60

Drop or swing-handled basket, nineteenth century, New England. $375–$450

White oak basket, hickory handle, c. 1940. $75–$100

Shaker basket, ash splint, New England, nineteenth century. $500–$650. *Below*, finely woven bottom.

Rare feather basket with slide lid, painted green. **$400–$500**

Rectangular market basket, New England, oak splint, possibly Shaker. **$375–$475**

Rectangular gathering basket, oak splint. **$75–$85**

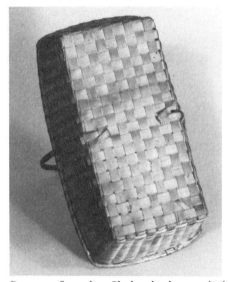

Bottom of another Shaker basket, typical of many sold by the Shakers to visitors to their New England communities.

Nantucket Lightship basket, rattan with turned pine bottom, late nineteenth century. **$600–$750**

Three Nantucket Lightship baskets of graduated size, New England, late nineteenth century. **$2400-$3000**, set

Oak splint basket, wrapped rim, carved handle. **$65-$80**

Feather or storage basket, white oak splint, painted, found in North Carolina. **$165-$200**

Winnowing basket, 39″ diameter, found in New York state. **$285-$325**

Uncommon double-handled basket with oval mouth and rectangular base. **$150–$175**

White oak splint buttocks basket with double handle. **$250–$300**

White oak gathering basket, early twentieth century. **$75–$85**

Native American ash "ribbon" basket, early twentieth century. **$140–$155**

Swing-handled market basket, possibly Shaker, New England. **$330–$385**

Painted oak splint basket, nineteenth century. **$300–$350**

Field basket used for gathering root crops, found in Illinois; 40″ diameter. **$400–$500**

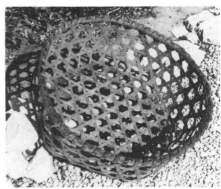

Splint cheese basket, 26″ diameter. **$550–$700**

Ash splint basket with drop or bail handle and "kicked in" bottom. **$375–$450**

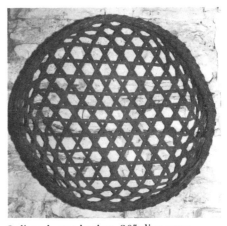

Splint cheese basket, 20″ diameter. **$500–$600**

Factory-made bushel basket with thick, wide splint and drop handle. **$95–$110**

Footed storage basket, oak splint, carved handles. **$150–$175**

133

8
Country Store Antiques

A New York state auction of advertising and country store collectibles in November 1987 brought record prices. An 1890s Yellow Kid Ginger Wafer tin from the New York Biscuit Company sold for $11,000. A Lime Kiln Club Smoking Tobacco tin was auctioned for $13,200. Both tins are exceptionally rare and few other examples are known.

It is critical to note that the tins were in exceptional condition. Unlike a piece of furniture that can be repaired and still maintain much of its value, condition is absolutely crucial in evaluating

Hiram Sibley seed box filled with original seed packets. **$350–$400**

country store antiques and collectibles. If a metal coffee bin has been repainted, or a seed box is found without its paper labels, the piece has minimal value.

Notes on Collecting

1. Signs, tin containers, wooden product boxes, and cast-iron counter coffee grinders can be found almost anywhere. Small grocery stores and general stores were found in every hamlet, village, and town by 1880.

2. Flea markets have long been an excellent source for items in quantity that turn up all at once. A box was recently found in the basement of a warehouse under demolition in Charlotte, North Carolina, filled with metal signs in perfect condition that extolled the virtues of a long-deceased chiropractor. The signs were sold a week later at the Metrolina Antiques Market. This is not an unusual happening.

3. Condition is essential to maintaining value. If an item has been repainted, reworked, or damaged, its value diminishes dramatically.

4. There are several regional antiques shows that contain only country store and advertising items. These are excellent opportunities to meet fellow collectors and to learn more about availability and price trends.

Stack of eight Shakers' seed boxes. **$6500–$7500**

Collection of seventeen product boxes with paper labels. **$2200–$2800**

Two packets of Sibley bean seeds. **$6–$8** each

Keen's Mustard box. **$140–$150**

Burbank Seed Company box. **$200–$225**

Northern Grown Seeds box. **$175–$200**

Northern Seeds box. **$200–$225**

Durkee Spices box. **$100–$125**

Seed jars from a country store with packet labels. **$18–$20** each

Hart's Seeds jar. **$10–$14**

Seed tins with colorful labels. **$14–$18** each

Oversized Burt "Sunrise" seed packets. **$9–$12** each

Rice's Flower Seeds box. **$75–$85**

Boxes of Burt Peas seed. **$4–$6** each

Shakers' seed box with rare interior label. **$800–$1000**

Shaker Garden Seed box, rare and early. **$1400–$1700**

Stickney and Poor's Mustard box, without lid. **$45–$60**

Stickney and Poor's Mustard box. **$125–$140**

Glass seed jars. **$24–$28** each

Reliable Seeds box. **$150–$175**

Mt. Lebanon Shakers Seeds box. **$700–$800**

Colburn's Mustard box. **$125–$145**

Miniature Ezra Williams seed box.
$250–$300

Chameleon Glycerin soap box. $75–85

John Gray tobacco box. $85–$100

Stickney and Poor's Mustard box.
$125–$140

Ezra Williams seed box. $275–$330

Mid-nineteenth century seed boxes.
$325–$425 each

Rice's Seeds. **$125–$150**

Somerset Garden Seeds boxes. **$225–$250** each

Hiram Sibley Seeds box. **$250–$300**

Stickney and Poor's box. **$125–$140**

Slade's Mustard box. **$135–$150**

Shaker "community" seed box from Alfred, Maine; blue paint. **$1000–$1200**

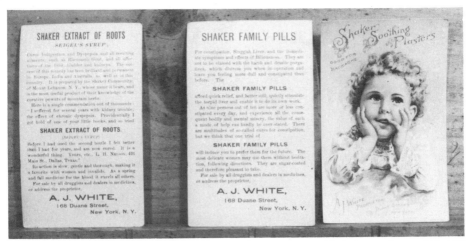

Shaker trade cards given out in New England stores that sold their products. **$30–$35** each

Rice's Seeds box. **$75–$85**

Product containers, c. 1900. **$10–$32** each

Lion Fancy Roasted Coffee package. **$15–$20**

Rice's Flower Seeds box, oak; **$75–$85**.
Individual boxes of seeds, **$6–$7** each.

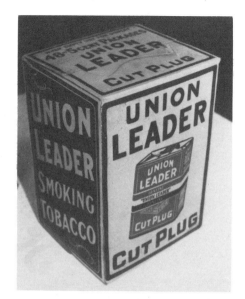

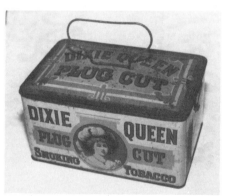

Dixie Queen plug cut tobacco tin.
$50–$65

Union Leader box for packages of tobacco. **$50–$60**

Green Turtle Cigars tin. **$75–$85**

Stoneware whiteroot bottle, molded.
$50–$65

Spool cabinet from country store, c. 1900.
$225–$300

Jell-O sign, paper. **$7–$9**

Choice Family Flour sack. **$8–$12**

Gold Band Roasted Coffee paper box.
$14–$16

Fishing sign, c. 1988. **$125–$150**

Tobacco tins. **$12–$20** each

Beech-Nut Chewing Tobacco counter display tin box. **$85–$115**

"Guest" sign from 1930s motor hotel. **$50–$75**

Purity Rolled Oats paper container. **$20–$25**

Wooden product boxes, from the 1920s and 1930s. **$55–$65** each

Cash register. **$65–$70**

Counter-size Dixie Queen tin without handle. **$25–$30**

Shoe lace display with clock. **$135–$150**

Luter's Pure Lard container with "drop" handle. **$45–$55**

Coca-Cola sidewalk sign. **$75–$100**

Tin haircut sign in pine frame. **$100–$175**

Luzianne Coffee containers. **$50–$55** each

Adriance Farm Machinery wooden sign. **$65–$75**

Coca-Cola machine, working condition. **$175–$225**

Mason's shoe polish box, "as found" condition. **$55–$60**

Yosemite Mills cinnamon box, without slide lid. **$50–$55**

Orange painted box with blue lettering, "Fritz, Covington, Ky." **$30–$35**

Apple butter bucket with label and "drop" handle. **$200–$250**

Cannister fire extinguishers. **$55–$60** each

Metal Putnam Dye cabinet, rough condition. **$60–$75**

Button's Raven Gloss Shoe Dressing box. **$125–$150**

Christmas sign from a bank, c. 1950. **$35–$45**

Barrel-type coffee bin. **$135–$175**

Red Comb Feeds sign, metal. **$35–$50**

Spool cabinet, original condition and finish. **$250–$375**

Shaker Pickles wooden crate. **$350–$425**

Atlas pine box. **$20–$25**

Counter display container for candy or nuts, refinished. **$85–$100**

Pal-O-Mine coffee tin. **$24–$28**

Utopia Cigars tin. **$50–$60**

John Ruskin Cigars tin. **$50–$55**

Red Drops tin. **$22–$28**

Model Smoking Tobacco sign. **$40–$45**

Daintie Soda Crackers tin. **$30–$35**

Sweet Mist Chewing Tobacco cylindrical container. **$85–$120**

Sweet Cuba Fine Cut Tobacco round tin. **$60–$75**

"Roly Poly" tobacco tins, first quarter of the twentieth century. Englishman, or Man from Scotland Yard, **$700–$800**; Dutchman, **$550–$675**.

Maryland Chief oyster cans, unopened. **$20–$28** each

Hickok's Marshmallows tin. **$35–$45**

Manewal-Lange Biscuit tin. **$18–$25**

Gun powder container. **$65–$75**

Union Leader Tobacco cannister.
$12–$18

Gold Dust washing powder box. **$50–$55**

Shot Gun Powder container. **$65–$75**

153

Yacht Club Marshmallow tin. **$15–$20**

Ehlers pepper barrel, used on a counter.
$120–$150

Chase and Sanborn's coffee tin, used on a
countertop. **$135–$150**

Quality Biscuit cardboard box (rare) and
metal overlay. **$45–$55**, box; **$15–$20**,
overlay

Columbia Cut Plug Smoking Tobacco.
$50–$55

Tin Rook playing cards container.
$12–$15

Big Sioux Biscuit tin. **$28–$32**

Kohrs Lard container. **$15–$18**

Tip Top cereal box. **$8–$10**

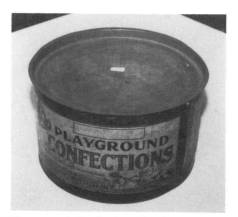

Playground Confections tin. **$30–$35**

Ojibwa tobacco tin. **$48–$60**

Empty tin cans with colorful labels. **$6–$8** each

Dilling's marshmallow tin. **$18–$22**

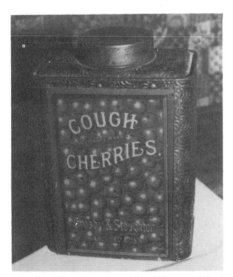

Cough Cherries tin with slide-out label. **$100–$125**

Velvet smoking tobacco tin. **$22–$24**

Cardboard "Biggest Sucker in Town" box. **$2–$3**

Rex marshmallows tin. **$15–$20**

First Aid Cabinet, c. 1930. **$95–$115**

Pepsi menu sign, metal. **$22–$26**

Canterbury Shakers candy box.
$100–$115

Barber shop sign from Baltimore hotel.
$400–$475

Wooden pie boxes with glass fronts for
counter display. **$75–$85** each

Santa Claus mailbox from Esso station. **$95–$115**

Spool cabinet. **$300–$325**

Paper sign. **$4–$5**

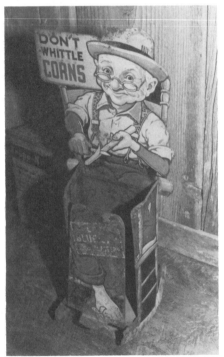

"Don't Whittle Corns" counter display, metal. **$55–$60**

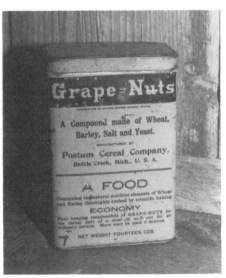

Grape-Nuts tin box. **$55–$65**

Virginia Dare sign. **$12–$20**

Tip Top bread storage box. **$150–$175**

Jewelry store sign, cast zinc. **$275–$400**

Baggage room wooden sign from Illinois railroad station, 6 feet long. **$150–$175**

Pepsi machine, working condition. **$275–$300**

Metal "Good Housekeeping" sign.
$35–$40

Metal outdoor sign pointing to Clay
Dooley tire store. **$45–$50**

Metal Faulkner's tobacco sign. **$38–$45**

Ted's Root Beer sign. **$15–$25** (1987)

Paper umbrellas. **$20–$25** each

"Painless Dentist" sign. **$20–$25**

No Trespassing wooden sign. **$35–$40**

Shaker brushes sold in New England communities. **$100–$125** each

Paper KC Baking Powder sign. **$18–$22**

Sunbeam steam iron holder. **$15–$20**

9
Potpourri

This section of each edition contains a wide spectrum of country antiques, ranging from stuffed chickens from Maine to windmill weights from Nebraska and the Dakotas. We have received letters recently from individuals who like this section of each edition best because it's filled with surprises.

We have never consciously collected anything in particular. When we go to antiques shows, we are never looking for a specific piece of furniture or a 3-gallon stoneware crock with a chicken pecking corn to its left. We look at everything

Soap Saver scrubbing board, c. 1930. **$45–$50**

and, if we like it and can afford it, we buy it.

Hopefully, the selection herein reflects that attitude.

Mechanical Banks

The "golden age" of mechanical banks extended from 1870 to approximately 1915. For a bank to have significant value today, it must be in working order, contain no replaced parts, and carry its original paint in almost perfect condition.

"Teddy and the Bear." **$1800–$2100**

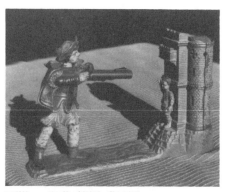

William Tell. **$750–$1100**

"Eagle and Eaglets." **$650–$800**

"Bad Accident." **$1300–$1650**

"Two Frogs." **$800–$1000**

Rabbit chocolate molds, early 1900s.
$75–$85

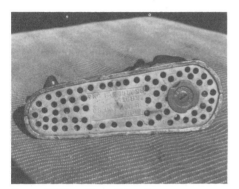

Base of "Two Frogs" bank.

Household Aids

Collection of tin cookie molds, c. 1900.
$8–$14 each

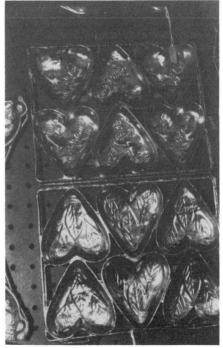

Heart chocolate molds, early 1900s.
$70–$80

Cast-iron coffee grinder with glass jar, early 1900s. **$55–$65**

Wire used to take canning jars in and out of water. **$5–$6**

Cast-iron iron with maple handle, early 1900s. **$24–$30**

Toaster from the early 1900s. **$20–$25**

Metal corn dryers, commonly found in Illinois and Indiana, c. 1930. **$12–$14** each

Factory-made chopping knives, early 1900s. **$9–$20** each

Copper wash boiler, c. 1920. **$75–$85**

Cast-iron raisin seeder. **$30–$40**

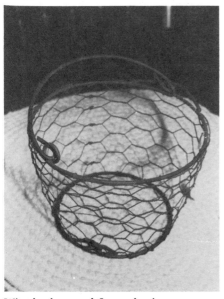

Wire basket used for gathering eggs. **$15–$17**

Rare pierced-tin food grater, c. 1840. **$135–$150**

Cast-iron "sad" irons. **$15–$24** each

Factory-made food graters, twentieth century. **$12–$14** each

Tin flour or sugar scoop, early 1900s. **$22–$24**

Brass cuspidor, c. 1890. **$100–$135**

Child's lunch box, c. 1950. **$12–$20**

Cast-iron Shaker stove, Mt. Lebanon, New York. **$600–$750**

Cast-iron fire alarm box, found in Chicago, Illinois; c. 1890. **$250–$300**

Gas stove from the 1920s. **$300–$400**

Metal bath tub, c. 1900. **$200–$225**

Kerosene lamp, early 1900s. **$55–$70**

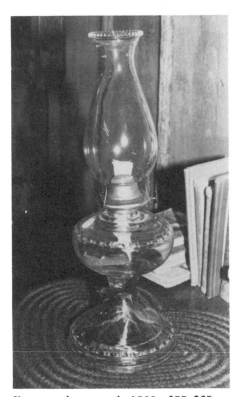

Kerosene lamp, early 1900s. **$55–$65**

Kerosene "sweet heart" lamps, early 1900s. **$135–$175** each

Kerosene barn lantern, early 1900s. **$85–$115**

Cast-iron "Hummer" windmill weight on ball. **$575–$675**

Kerosene railroad lanterns. **$55–$70** each

Cast-iron squirrel windmill weight. **$1200–$1500**

Cast-iron "rainbow tail" windmill weight. **$1000–$1300**

Nineteenth century candle lanterns, factory made. Larger lantern, **$150–$200**; skater's lantern, **$125–$150**.

Copper candy kettles, dovetailed bottoms, iron handles. **$225–$250**

Circular twelve-tube candle mold, rare form, c. 1850. **$1000–$1200**

Candle lantern, late nineteenth century. **$125–$150**

Dazey butter churn. **$50–$55**

Refinished butter churn with wooden bands and a piggen handle, first half of the nineteenth century. **$400–$475**

Maple butter print, machine stamped strawberry decoration. **$95–$115**

Rare Pennsylvania German butter stamp, mortised construction, first half of the nineteenth century. **$400–$500**

Butter worker used to "work" water out of freshly churned butter, factory made, early 1900s. **$100–$130**

Factory-made butter churn, original painted finish and stencilled decoration, c. 1890. **$200–$250**

Butter churn, pine, original painted finish. **$95–$120**

"Barrel" butter churn, original painted finish, pine. **$75–$85**

Painted knife and fork boxes, pine, **$65–$75** each

Painted flax wheel, c. 1860. **$150–$200**

Painted butter churn, dasher type, wooden bands, New England, c. 1850. **$475–$550**

Pine tool box, painted, early twentieth century. **$55–$65**

Refinished factory-turned wooden bowl, early 1900s. **$55–$60**

Refinished knife and fork box with unusual base, c. 1875. **$85–$115**

Early twentieth century knife and fork box, pine, 9″ diameter, refinished. **$45–$55**

Wooden clip used to take fruit jars from boiling water, ash, factory made, early 1900s. **$5–$7**

Wood tends to crack or split across its grain as it shrinks. Wooden bowls are often found with cracks or splits. If a bowl is painted blue, yellow, green, or red, the price escalates dramatically. This "put together" nest of unpainted bowls is worth **$130–$150**.

Three factory-made bowls from the late nineteenth century. **$330–$350**, nest of three

Butter scoop, maple, handcarved, late nineteenth century, refinished. **$90–$115**

Hand-carved wooden bowl, nineteenth century. **$100–$125**

Painted mortars and pestles, maple, lathe turned, c. 1870. **$140–$175** each

Factory-made coffee grinder, machine dovetailed corners, maple, refinished. **$75–$85**

Factory-made coffee mill or grinder, c. 1900, original finish. **$100–$115**

Swift used for winding yarn, possibly Shaker but incomplete. **$100–$125**

Wooden factory-made clothes pins, twentieth century. **$1–$2** each

Swift, early twentieth century. **$100–$125**

Painted sugar bucket with "drop" handle and wooden "button hole" hoops, New England. **$250–$300**

Painted pantry boxes, factory produced, early twentieth century. **$85–$110** each

Blue sugar bucket, found without a lid, c. 1880. **$75–$85**; **$300–$325** with original lid

Refinished sugar bucket, factory made, wooden bands, early 1900s. **$85–$115**

Cigar mold, early 1900s. **$20–$24**

Unusual table with chipped, carved base, c. 1900. **$200–$250**

Pantry boxes with "drop" handles, painted, early twentieth century. **$135–$150** each

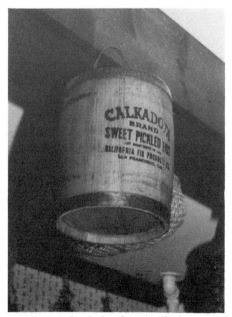

Small staved tub for figs, c. 1930s. **$15–$18**

Graniteware
and Tinware

Graniteware, also known as *enamelware*, *agateware*, *porcelainware*, *glazedware*, or *speckleware*, was popular from the 1860s until the early 1930s, when the mass marketing of aluminum products destroyed the market.

The graniteware and tinware items that follow were factory made from about 1890 until the 1930s. They are not exceptional examples, but they are still underpriced and highly collectible.

$20–$24

$55–$65

$20–$35

$20–$25

$65–75

FLOUR

$55–$65

$20–$30

$20–$28 each

$20–$30

$15–$18

$18–$22

$60–$65

$24–$28

$175–$225

Bread Boards and Knives

$12–$18

Factory-made bread knives with maple handles, c. 1920. **$30–$35** each

Factory-made bread boards, maple, first quarter of the twentieth century. **$35–$45**

Bread board, c. 1910. **$35–$50**

Bread board with impressed or stamped decoration. **$35–$50**

The boards were turned on a lathe and then steamed to make the maple pliable. The designs on the boards were stamped or impressed mechanically. **$35–$50**

Bread knives and plates were listed in Wards' and Sears' catalogs into the 1930s. In recent years, there have been numerous reproductions. **$35–$50**, boards; **$30–$35**, knives.

Maple bread board with stamped decoration and "Bread" hand-carved on side. **$35–$50**

Washday Antiques

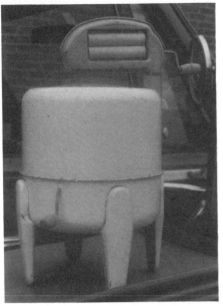

Child's washing machine, c. 1940s.
$85–$115

National Washboard Company scrub board, c. 1930. **$20–$25**

Staved wooden washing machine, pine with iron bands, c. 1890. **$150–$175**

National Washboard with metal surface, c. 1940. **$25–$30**

Lingerie wash board, metal scrubbing surface, c. 1920. **$40–$45**

Wooden washing machine, c. 1890; pine, original finish. **$150–$175**

Metal scrubbing board with wooden legs, c. 1900. **$45–$55**

Ceramic scrubbing board in wooden frame, c. 1900. **$75–$85**

Maid-Rite board with metal scrubbing surface and maple frame. **$40–$45**

Pine washing machine, original worn finish, iron bands, c. 1890–1910. **$150–$175**

Copper wash boiler, "as found" condition. **$30–$35**

Standard Family Size washboard with brass surface and maple frame, c. 1930. **$35–$45**

$135–$150

Soap Saver scrub board, rare blue enamel, c. 1930. $75–$85

Spice Boxes

The spice boxes in this section were all factory made between 1880 and 1920. They were sold by the thousands through a variety of mail-order and catalog businesses. To maintain any significant value, a spice box must have its original finish and as much of the original lettering on the drawers as possible. The boxes may be found in wood or metal.

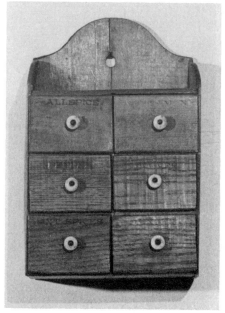

$225–$250

$125–$175

$175–$200

This is an exceptional spice chest with only one major problem: at some point, a misguided collector began refinishing the drawer at lower right. Once the process begins, the box cannot be restored and must be refinished—with a resulting significant decline in value and desirability.

$200–$225

$150–$175

Tin spice chest in original gold paint and lettering, c. 1890. **$250–$275**

$150–$175

Tin spice box with original paint and decoration, c. 1900. **$250–$300**

Toys and Playthings

Infant's "push" sled, early 1900s.
$85–$100

Handcrafted railroad engine, c. 1930, painted. **$75–$90**

Heavily worn or "loved" teddy bear, c. 1930s, unmarked. **$65–$75**

Youth sled, painted and stencilled decoration, c. 1900, Paris, Maine. **$125–$150**

Doll cradle. **$55–$65**

Victorian baby carriage, c. 1880.
$150–$175

Worn teddy bear, replaced eyes and nose,
c. 1930. **$100–$150**

Platform rocking horse, c. 1880; original
paint and condition, found at a farm sale
in central Illinois. **$375–$475**

Child's sleigh, c. 1900, painted.
$200–$225

Early 1900s copy of *The Night Before Christmas*. **$35–$45**

Doll cradle, painted pine with heart cutout, late nineteenth century. **$135–$150**

Collection of teddy bears. **$125–$450** each

Child's coverlet from the 1840s, Ohio.
$400–$500

Wicker baby carriages, c. 1920. **$375–
$450** each

Child's book, *Billy Whiskers*. **$25–$30**

Child's book of *Robinson Crusoe*, early
1900s. **$25–$30**

Child's three-wheel bicycle, c. 1940.
$100–$120

Victorian dollhouse, factory made, c. 1890. **$300–$385**

Kraft Circus Zoo, c. 1950s. **$50–$60**

Child's sleds, c. 1940s. **$20–$24** each

Stuffed monkey doll, c. 1940s. **$35–$45**

Pedal tractor from the 1950s. **$100–$125**

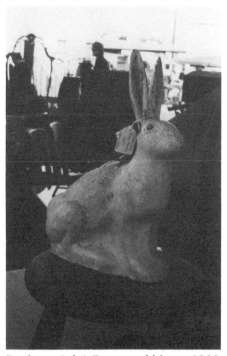

Papier mâché Easter rabbit, c. 1900. **$130–$160**

Papier mâché Easter rabbit, early 1900s. **$125–$150**

Rag doll, black woman with wooden legs and feet, 10″ tall, c. 1930–1940. **$25–$30**

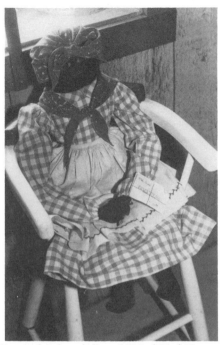

Reproduction doll, c. 1988. **$30–$40**

Golliwog doll, made of material and felt, 18″ tall, English, c. 1930s–1940s. **$45–$85**

Sheboygan Truck wagon with detachable side panels, c. 1930s. **$275–$325**

Railroad engine "ride" toy, original paint, excellent condition, c. 1940. **$200–$285**

A Medley of Collectibles

Copper and brass mold, possibly English, nineteenth century. **$225–$300**

Pine wheelbarrow, painted, c. 1920, iron wheels. **$135–$150**

Open carriage, c. 1900, working condition. **$750–$1000**

Hay rake, early twentieth century. **$100–$125**

Wheelchair, early 1900s. **$85–$100**

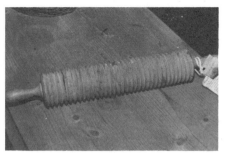

Wooden pin for rolling noodles, maple, factory made. **$55–$65**

Wooden spade made from one piece of wood. **$95–$115**

Whiskey barrels. **$25–$28** each

Potato masher, factory made, maple, original condition. **$18–$22**

Oversized bird hotel, "as found" condition. **$55–$70**

Birdhouse from the 1940s. **$75–$85**

Unusual birdhouse with steps, painted, c. 1940s. **$75–$80**

Black man clock, wooden face on metal clock, c. 1925. **$250–$350**

Alligator and boy highly glazed ceramic bank, c. 1940s–1950s. **$25–$35**

Octagon schoolhouse clock, c. early
1900s. **$350–$450**

Regulator schoolhouse clock, oak, c. 1910.
$375–$425

Unusual pine bucket-type bench used as a
washbowl with drain, robin's-egg-blue
paint, Illinois, late nineteenth century.
$1000–$1200

Sunburst decoration from Pennsylvania
barn, late nineteenth century.
$850–$1200

Pine tool box on bootjack legs, never painted, "as found" condition. **$55–$60**

Pine checkerboard, painted, original condition. **$200–$250**

Shoemaker's forms, maple, variety of sizes. **$7–$9** each

Rare checkerboard with star decorations, mid-nineteenth century. **$850–$1200**

Coverlet, c. 1840. **$450–$550**

Pine checkerboard, dated 1907, strong color. **$350–$425**

Final
Exam

W e have carried you through too many of these examinations. Your parents, or someone pretending to be your parents, has repeatedly telephoned and begged for one more chance. There will be no more chances. If you do not do well this time, no bookstore in America — with a single exception — will allow you to purchase this book.

There is an adult bookstore in Troyer, Nebraska, that will sell the book to you, but our regional testing center in Omaha will not certify the score.

Factory-made wooden spice box, original lettering and finish intact.
$175–$200

Questions

Read each question carefully and select the most appropriate response.

1. The handcrafted country cupboard in Fig. 1 dates from the middle nineteenth century.

   true   false

2. It is within the realm of possibility that this cupboard/cabinet could have been purchased from Sears and Roebuck in 1915.

   true   false

3. The cupboard in Fig. 1 appears to be made of pine.

   true   false

4. What is the approximate value of this piece?

   a. $300–$375
   b. $600–$750
   c. $1000–$1250
   d. more than $1250

5. More pieces of American country furniture are made of _____ than of any other wood.

   a. oak
   b. pine
   c. walnut
   d. maple

6. A cupboard with solid wooden doors can be described as a "_____" front.

7. A cupboard with glass in the doors typically is more difficult to find than a comparable example with solid wooden doors.

   true   false

Fig. 1

Fig. 2

8. Two dry sinks were pulled out of a barn. One was pine and the other was oak. Which is *probably* the older of the two?

9. The terms "original" paint and "early" paint are synonymous.

   true   false

10. The chair in Fig. 2 dates from approximately

    a. 1800–1830
    b. 1840–1860
    c. 1870–1900
    d. after 1920

11. It is highly probable that the chair in Fig. 2 is made entirely of pine.

    true   false

12. The stretchers are "dovetailed" into the legs of the chair.

    true   false

13. The original seat of the chair in Fig. 2 was constructed of:

    a. a pine plank
    b. rattan
    c. splint
    d. rush

14. The chair in Fig. 2, in its current condition, is worth approximately:

    a. less than $75
    b. $85–$125
    c. $150–$175
    d. more than $175

15. The chair could be described as a _____ -back.

Fig. 3

16. The pie safe in Fig. 3 appears to have been made in a factory.

    true   false

17. What is the approximate value of the pie safe "as found"?

    a. $100–$125
    b. $225–$300
    c. $350–$500
    d. more than $1000

18. Could this safe have been made after 1900?

    yes   no

19. Three of the four kinds of wood listed below were commonly used in the construction of pie safes. Select the wood that would have been the *least* likely to be used.

a. oak
b. maple
c. walnut
d. pine

20. Rank the colors below in the order that would add the most to the value of the painted pie safe in Fig. 3.

blue
brown
red
pink
yellow

21. Buckets similar to the ones in Fig. 4 served a single purpose. How were they used?

22. The buckets in Fig. 4 are held together by metal bands and have wooden _____.

23. The buckets date from the early 1800s.

true   false

24. The buckets are typically priced about:

a. $75–$100 each
b. $20–$35 each
c. $125–$150 each

25. The "5" on the churn in Fig. 5 is a _____ mark.

26. The "5" was:

a. put on the churn with a stencil
b. put on the churn with a brush
c. incised into the wet clay
d. none of the above

27. This churn dates from c. 1840–1860.

true   false

Fig. 4

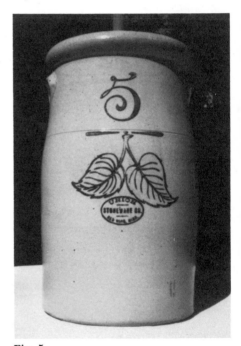

Fig. 5

28. The tool box in Fig. 6 is made of _____.

210

Fig. 6

Fig. 8

Fig. 7

29. If it were refinished, the value of the toolbox would decrease.

　　true　　false

30. This tool box in blue paint is worth about:

　　a. $25–$40
　　b. $85–$125
　　c. more than $200

31. The collection of stoneware in Fig. 7:

a. is incredible and worth thousands of dollars
b. could probably be purchased for less than $150
c. is the one you read about in USA Today. It was found in the basement of an abandoned stoneware factory near Cooperstown, New York in February, 1988
d. none of the above

32. The designs on the stoneware appear to have been executed with a brush.

　　true　　false

33. The painted box in Fig. 8 is made of:

a. walnut
b. oak
c. maple
d. pine

211

Fig. 9

34. The handles on the side appear to be hand-forged.

    true   false

35. What is the primary difference between a chest and a box?

36. A collector could expect to pay more than $785 for a comparable painted box.

    true   false

37. The piece of furniture in Fig. 9 could be best described as a

    _____.

38. It has been refinished and appears to have been constructed of walnut.

    true   false

39. This piece would date from the second half of the nineteenth century.

    true   false

40. What is the approximate value of the piece?

    a. $75–$125
    b. $150–$185
    c. $275–$400
    d. more than $400

41. A "light" could be found in the door of a glazed cupboard.

    true   false

42. Most pre-1850 stoneware was incised.

    true   false

43. The Erie Canal began outside Cleveland and meandered to Albany, N.Y.

    true   false

44. Shaker rocking chairs were made for sale to the "world" in at least ten sizes.

    true   false

45. The Museum of American Folk Art is located in Los Angeles.

    true   false

46. Most butter molds and prints are made of maple.

    true   false

Match the nationally known antiques markets below to the states in which they are held.

47. ___ Brimfield   a. Mich.

48. ___ Black Angus   b. Ill.

49. ___ Ann Arbor   c. Mass.

50. ___ 3rd Sunday   d. Pa.

Fig. 10

We used a picture of this gentleman's brother in an earlier edition of this book. Who is this guy?

a. Ronald Roop
b. Alfredo Blackwolfe
c. Alan Weintraub
d. Wayne Wills
e. none of the above

Answers

1. false
2. true
3. false
4. B is fairly realistic. We have seen them on the West Coast for more than $1000, and in the Midwest and Southeast for $200–400.
5. b
6. "blind"
7. true
8. The one made of pine.
9. false
10. c
11. false
12. false
13. c
14. a
15. slat-back or ladder-back
16. true
17. c
18. yes
19. b
20. blue, yellow, red, brown, pink
21. as sap buckets
22. staves
23. false—much closer to 1900 than 1800
24. b
25. capacity

26. a
27. false
28. pine
29. true
30. b
31. d
32. false (a slip-cup)
33. d
34. false
35. A chest has drawers.
36. false
37. commode
38. false
39. true
40. c
41. true
42. false
43. false
44. false
45. false (New York City)
46. true
47. c
48. d
49. a
50. b

Bonus Question
d—none of the above

Scoring Scale

46–50 With this score and a letter of reference from a randomly selected used car salesman from Yonkers, New York, you are eligible for admission to most of the barber colleges in Mississippi.

41–45 With work you could become one of the all-time great national authorities. Based on your psychological profile and résumé in our file, you won't.

36–40 We gave a test booklet and pencil to 33 monkeys at the St. Louis Zoo. After one hour we gathered the tests. The average score of the 29 monkeys who completed the exercise was 38. Draw your own conclusions.

35–39 Give serious consideration to spending time with another hobby. You might want to begin a collection of indoor-outdoor carpeting, paper placemats, hospital sheets, or Tupperware.